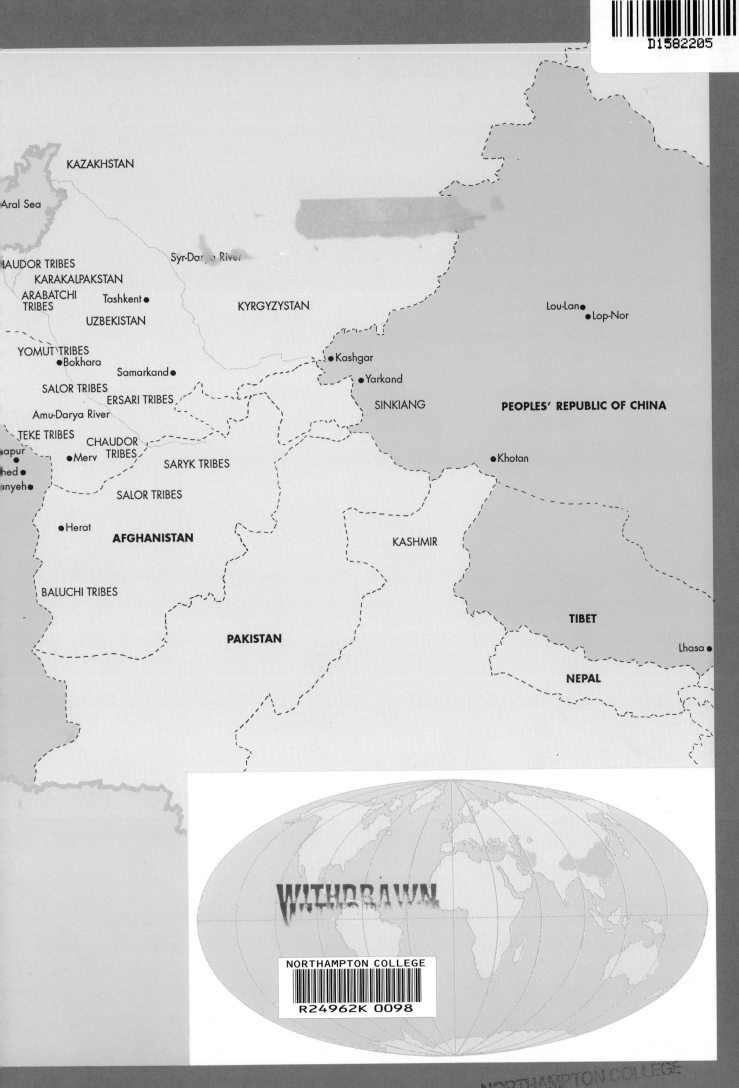

KAZAKHSTAN

Aral Sea

HAUDOR TRIBES

Syr-Darya River

KARAKALPAKSTAN

ARABATCHI
TRIBES

Tashkent ●

KYRGYZYSTAN

UZBEKISTAN

Lou-Lan ●
● Lop-Nor

YOMUT TRIBES
● Bokhara

Samarkand ●

● Kashgar

SALOR TRIBES

● Yarkand

ERSARI TRIBES

SINKIANG

PEOPLES' REPUBLIC OF CHINA

Amu-Darya River

TEKE TRIBES

CHAUDOR
TRIBES

apur

● Merv

hed ●

SARYK TRIBES

● Khotan

anyeh ●

SALOR TRIBES

● Herat

AFGHANISTAN

KASHMIR

BALUCHI TRIBES

TIBET

Lhasa ●

PAKISTAN

NEPAL

WITHDRAWN

NORTHAMPTON COLLEGE

R24962K 0098

NORTHAMPTON COLLEGE
LIBRARY

D1582205

ORIENTAL RUGS

Afshar rug c. 1880

JOHN J. COLLINS JR. GALLERY

ORIENTAL RUGS

THE COLLECTOR'S GUIDE TO SELECTING, IDENTIFYING, AND ENJOYING NEW AND VINTAGE ORIENTAL RUGS

George O'Bannon

AN IMPRINT OF RUNNING PRESS
PHILADELPHIA • LONDON

A QUINTET BOOK

Copyright © 1995 Quintet Publishing Limited.
All rights reserved under the Pan American and
International Copyright Conventions. This book may
not be reproduced in whole or in part, in any form or
by any means, electronic or mechanical, including
photocopying, recording, or by any information
storage and retrieval system now known or hereafter
invented, without written permission from the
Publisher and copyright holder.

Canadian Representatives:
General Publishing Co., Ltd.
30 Lesmill Road, Don Mills
Ontario M3B 2T6

9 8 7 6 5 4 3 2 1
Digit on the right indicates the number of this printing

Library of Congress
Cataloguing-in-Publication Number
94–73878

ISBN 1–56138–528–X

This book was designed and produced by
Quintet Publishing Limited
6 Blundell Street
London N7 9BH

Creative Director: Richard Dewing
Designer: Ian Hunt
Project Editor: Claire Tennant-Scull
Editor: Ruth Baldwin
Photographer: Gary McKinnis

Typeset in Great Britain by
Central Southern Typesetters, Eastbourne
Manufactured in Hong Kong by
Regent Publishing Services Ltd.
Printed in China by Leefung-Asco Printers Limited

AUTHOR'S ACKNOWLEDGMENTS

The author wishes to thank the following individuals
and businesses who provided photographs from their
collections or inventories: Peter Pap Oriental Rugs,
Inc., Dublin, NH and San Francisco, CA; John J.
Collins, Jr. Gallery, Newburyport, MA; George Fine
Kelims, Tuscon, AZ; George Jevremovic, Woven
Legends, Inc., Philadelphia, PA; Kesang Tashi,
InnerAsia Trading Co., New York, NY; Chris Walter,
Yayla Tribal Rugs, Cambridge, MA; Teddy Sumner,
Black Mountain Looms, Inc., New York, NY;
Zollanvari AG, Zurich; Michael Scott, Return to
Tradition, San Francisco, CA; Brian and Stephanie
Morehouse; Dennis and Maile Marquand and
numerous private collectors who wish to remain
anonymous. I especially thank Gary McKinnis for his
photographic skill and patience in seeing this project
to fruition.

The Azeri, DOBAG and Ersari rugs on pages 66
through to page 73 are trademarked names.

Published by Courage Books
an imprint of Running Press Book Publishers
125 South Twenty-second Street
Philadelphia, Pennsylvania 19103–4399

CONTENTS

JOHN J. COLLINS JR. GALLERY.

INTRODUCTION

This book is a brief and general introduction to Oriental rugs and is intended as a guide to those who might wish to collect them. It is not about how to buy such a rug for use in your home. Rather it is intended for people who have already purchased a rug and been captivated by its artistry, charm, and unique characteristics and who may wish to know what they must learn to become a knowledgeable collector.

To appreciate Oriental rugs more fully you need to know something of the characteristics of weave, design, lifestyle of the rug weavers, and how the rugs of one country differ from those of another. The purpose of this book is to present some of these for the potential collector. So many designs and patterns have been created throughout the rug-weaving areas that reliance on them alone is unwise. Thus emphasis is placed on the structure of rugs as a method of identification. Structure and design must be used together if you are to begin to learn about Oriental rugs.

A BRIEF HISTORY OF THE ORIENTAL CARPET

It is not known just when the weaving of rugs began. The oldest carpet in existence is the Pazyryk carpet, which was found frozen in a burial tomb in Inner Asia and is dated to the fourth century B.C. Its design, dyes, and weave are all of the highest quality, indicating that the weaver was knowledgeable and experienced. From this carpet and other data, it is assumed that rug weaving must have evolved by the second millennium B.C.

Records and evidence of carpet weaving from the Pazyryk to the fourteenth century are fragmentary. Some rug remnants from the third, sixth, and eleventh centuries survive, but without any connection or continuity. A continuous connection for rugs from Anatolia exists from the fourteenth century and for

ABOVE LEFT **The red and yellow arabesque of this Bijar rug defines an all-over design** **creating areas containing floral and plant patterns.**

ABOVE **Detail of a Shusha carpet illustrating the wide color range of this group. The pattern is a simplified version of the mina khani pattern.**

RIGHT **Detail of a Sarouk carpet with floral medallions consisting of floral sprays, palmettes, rosettes, and leaf forms.**

Persia from the sixteenth century. Thus the study of Oriental rugs covers only the last five hundred years with any great degree of certainty.

Oriental carpets have been used and collected in the West for centuries. Our knowledge of them is based primarily on their depiction in religious and court paintings from the fifteenth century onward. The earliest of these are religious paintings in which the rugs typically are shown under a throne on which the Virgin Mary is seated. By the sixteenth century, rugs begin to appear in the paintings of royalty on tables or under the feet of a sovereign to emphasize his power, importance, and wealth. The types of rugs depicted in these paintings have acquired the names of the painters, such as Holbein, Memling, Crivelli, Lotto.

With the development of sea routes to the East increasing numbers of rugs became available to and were acquired by the expanding wealthy merchant classes of Europe. The Dutch particularly were fond of Oriental rugs and they are frequently included, primarily as table covers, in Dutch genre paintings of the seventeenth century. The presence of rugs in paintings is one of the principal ways of dating the relatively few carpets remaining from before the

nineteenth century. In them it is possible to study the evolution of various designs and place the rugs into periods and groups.

Prior to the seventeenth century almost all of these rugs are from the area we know today as Turkey. However, during that century rugs from Persia begin to appear because the European states were trading with the Safavid Empire and many goods were reaching Europe via the Silk Road, which passed through Persia. Although there were ups and downs in this trade, Persia remained one of the principal sources of Oriental carpets from then on.

The Oriental rug languished as a luxury and decorative item from the mid-1700s until the mid-1800s. With the expansion of the middle class in Europe and America by the mid-nineteenth century, however, there was a rebirth of interest in Oriental rugs. This led to a revival and expansion of rug weaving in Turkey, the Caucasus, Persia, Central Asia, India, and China. Most of the rugs that are prized by collectors today were woven after this time. These are the rugs on which this book is focused. The various types that have been collected, are being collected and may be collected in the future are described here.

JOHN J. COLLINS JR. GALLERY.

THE CRAFT OF CARPET MAKING

CHAPTER **1**

Many factors go into the making of a rug and knowing what they are helps in identifying the rug. The knot, type of loom, size, and patterns together indicate where, why, by whom, and how it was woven. You must learn something about these aspects to understand not only the language of Oriental rug collecting but also how to distinguish between the various types.

HOW RUGS ARE MADE

All Oriental rugs, to be classified as such, must be handmade. Beyond that they are made of different types of wool, on different types of loom, with many types of dye, in a wide array of patterns, and under many different circumstances. All of these factors combined tell something about a rug and aid in its identification.

STRUCTURAL TERMINOLOGY Rugs are made of essentially three types of thread: the warp, weft and pile. Each serves a specific function.

The *warp* is wrapped on the loom and is the foundation thread of a rug. The warp is usually exposed as the fringe. Warps at the side of a rug are finished in special ways to create an edge.

The *weft* is inserted sinuously across the width of the loom, perpendicular or at right angles to the warp, and after each row of knots to hold them in place. It binds all the threads into a cohesive structure.

The *pile* or *knot* creates the pattern. There are two types of pile knot, *symmetric* and *asymmetric*. Older names for the symmetric knot are Turkish, Ghiordes, and double; and for the asymmetric, Persian, Senneh, and single. The asymmetric knot may be tied to open

ABOVE LEFT **A Bijar carpet c. 1880 clearly illustrating what is meant by persianate patterns, with a herati pattern in the main field and extravagant** **arabesques overlapping in the border. Note that the main and secondary borders are reconciled at the top and unreconciled at the bottom.**

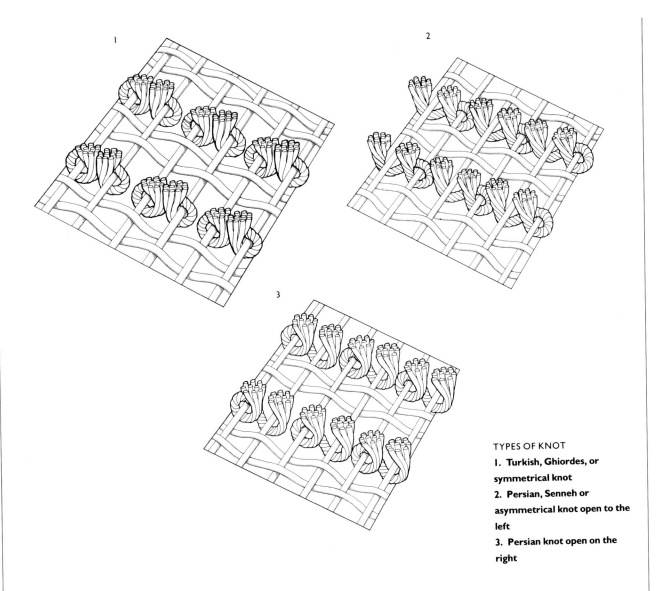

TYPES OF KNOT
1. **Turkish, Ghiordes, or symmetrical knot**
2. **Persian, Senneh or asymmetrical knot open to the left**
3. **Persian knot open on the right**

right or open left. Each type of knot can also be woven to give the pile an inclination to the right or left.

Warp depression refers to the way in which the warps can be made to lie parallel to one another or on different levels. It is done by manipulating the wefts. Warp depression increases knot density.

Knot density refers to the number of knots in a specific square unit of measurement: for example, square inches. Knots are counted vertically and horizontally within the given area on the back of the rug and the horizontal and vertical counts are multiplied to get the number of knots per square measure. Horizontally the two nodes at the base of the knot are counted as one knot. Vertically one node between each row of wefts represents a knot. The most common error of beginners is to count the two horizontal nodes as two knots.

This counting method applies only to rugs with warps on one level. Counting depressed warps requires more knowledge.

Knot density is a reflection of many aspects of a rug's construction, such as size of the warp, weft, and pile threads, how tightly the weaver tamps each row of knots and the presence or absence of warp depression. Knot density is not the determinant of quality. Most rugs of a type fall within a certain knot density. A type of rug noted for high knot density is not better than one with medium knot density; it is probably more expensive, but not better. Cost, not aesthetic merit, wool quality, or rarity, is most closely correlated with knot density.

9

NORTHAMPTON COLLEGE
LIBRARY

MATERIALS Rug weavers use many types of fiber. The most common are wool and cotton. Silk, camelhair, goathair, and horsehair are uncommon.

Wool is the most common fiber and is used for the warp, weft, and pile. It is dyed and used to create patterns. Natural wool colors used are white, gray, tan, dark brown, and black. Types of wool vary in luster, durability, and feel.

Cotton, the next most common fiber, is mainly used for the warp and weft. It is infrequently found in the pile, but when so used is an important identification factor. Cotton is white unless dyed.

Silk is the most expensive fiber used in rugs and may be used for warp, weft, and pile. Its use is a sign of opulence and, because it can be spun more finely than wool or cotton, it is often found in the most finely knotted rugs. Silk may be used in its natural off-white color or dyed.

Camelhair is used mostly as a pile thread in its natural color, which may vary from pale tan to brown.

Goathair and *horsehair* are used mostly for the edges of rugs; they are more durable than the other fibers. These fibers are dark brown or black.

TYPES OF LOOM Looms vary considerably in their construction. The following brief descriptions are intended to illustrate the two principal types.

The *horizontal* loom is constructed parallel to the ground and is the simpler of the two types. It consists of two beams around which the warp threads are wrapped. It is raised slightly off the ground, and the weaver sits on top of the warp threads to weave. This loom is easily portable and can be moved with an unfinished weaving on it. Rugs woven on horizontal looms commonly do not have perfectly equal sides and ends.

The *vertical* loom is constructed vertical to the ground. It may be made as a freestanding loom that can be leaned against a wall or built permanently in place. The weaver sits in front of the loom to weave. This loom can have complex structural features and is not readily portable. Rugs woven on vertical looms have sides and ends more equal in measurement.

DYES IN RUGS

Prior to the discovery of the first synthetic dye in 1856, the dyes in Oriental rugs came from natural sources. With the rapid development of synthetic dyes and their quick acceptance throughout the world, they were being adopted by Oriental rug weavers by the 1860s, though natural dyes continued to be used for several decades. By the beginning of the twentieth century, however, synthetic dyes had almost totally displaced natural ones. To understand why certain Oriental rugs are considered desirable and others are not, it is necessary to gain some understanding of what these various types of dye were and their effect on the weavings.

NATURAL DYES came from plants, minerals and insects. For plant dyes, any part of a plant could be used – flowers, leaves, stems or roots. Some of the most common natural dye sources are outlined below.

For red, madder was the most common plant source; it is a warm red because of the yellow components in its make-up. Cochineal was derived from several species of scale insects; it is a cool red because of the blue components in its makeup. Other red dyes were derived from safflower and brazilwood, but these were never as important in rugs as madder and cochineal.

Yellow dyes came from the most diverse plant sources. Saffron crocus stamens, pomegranate rind, dyer's weed, larkspur, camomile, salvia, and certain sumacs all provided yellows.

Indigo was the source for blue: this source yields all shades. Walnut and oak trees provided many browns with the husks of their fruit. The browns varied from mid to dark shades. Most browns, because of their tannic acid content, are corrosive, causing the fibers to become brittle and wear more quickly. In general this is not considered a negative feature because it results in an etched effect. Natural brown wool was also used.

Green resulted from combining indigo with a yellow dye. Many naturally produced greens are more of a blue-green. True greens are scarce, but do exist. Many greens become blue-green with time as the yellow component fades.

Orange resulted primarily from combining red and yellow dyes. Some orange-red shades resulted from the use of weakened madder dye baths.

Many colors in the violet/purple range resulted from combining a red and indigo. Some are the result of a special treatment of madder.

Black was usually produced from a combination of a tannic dye, such as oak acorn husks or pomegranate tree galls, with iron salts. As with brown dyes, black is corrosive, only more so.

MORDANTS For most dyes to adhere or fix themselves to wool fiber, the wool must first be treated with a metallic salt, called a mordant. This metallic salt may be iron, aluminum, copper, or tin. The type and strength of the mordant used not only fixes the dye but

affects the color tone as well. For example, iron mordants can make a madder dye rust in tone, while tin will make it clear and bright. Indigo and the brown dyes do not require mordants. For this reason they are called direct dyes.

SYNTHETIC DYES were accidentally discovered by William H. Perkin, an eighteen-year-old English chemistry student, in 1856 and were produced from coal tar. The first synthetic dye, called mauvine, was quickly followed by two others named fuchine and magenta. As a group these first synthetics were called aniline dyes. The Germans developed a type called azo dyes. Thus in Oriental rug literature references can be found to these dyes as coal tar, aniline, and azo.

The dyes were exported to the East and, as already mentioned, were used in Oriental rugs by the 1860s. The synthetic dyes available then were reds, oranges, yellows, and greens; synthetic indigo was not discovered until 1897.

Rug literature contains many references to the deleterious effects of synthetic dyes, the most common being fading and bleeding. Some of the reds were notorious for bleeding and the magentas, pinks, and greens faded considerably. There were, however, some synthetic dyes that neither faded nor bled: a particularly vivid orange is a case in point, which most Oriental rug collectors quickly learn to recognize and avoid.

At the beginning of the twentieth century a new group of chrome mordant synthetic dyes came into being. They did not have the problems of bleeding and fading suffered by the early synthetics. After World War I, chrome dyes began to be used in Oriental rug weaving along with the aniline and azo dyes, though it was not until the 1950s that they came to dominate the industry.

PETER PAP ORIENTAL RUGS, INC. PHOTO GARY McKINNIS.

LEFT **This Perepedil Kuba rug c. 1880 was dyed with early synthetic dyes except for the indigo. The colors have faded either naturally or were treated with a chemical wash.**

HOW TO DISTINGUISH BETWEEN NATURAL AND SYNTHETIC DYES The only sure way to tell whether a dye is natural or synthetic is by laboratory analysis. However, most collectors learn to use the eye test. This is a skill that comes only with seeing many Oriental rugs and having certain colors, fading, and bleeding pointed out. It is always fallible.

One of the visual differences between natural and synthetic dyes is the way in which they penetrate the fibers in a skein of wool. Natural dyes show subtle gradations of color within the thread; synthetic dyes penetrate the fibres evenly, giving the same depth of color throughout. The pile of a rug knotted with natural dyes shows color variances; synthetic dyes are even and uniform.

With exposure to light and use, natural and synthetic dyes both change but in different ways. Synthetic dyes fade; natural dyes soften and mellow – and there is a difference. New natural-dyed rugs can have the same harsh look of new synthetic-dyed ones. As natural dyes soften, however, they do not change to another color. When synthetic dyes fade, they become another color: for instance, magenta becomes gray, dark green turns chartreuse. If they do not fade, as most chrome dyes do not, they maintain the same intensity as on the day when they were woven.

To confirm the degree of fading, fold a rug to see the base of the knot. If a natural dye was used, the color will be essentially uniform from the tip of the knot to the base. If it is a fading synthetic dye, the tip and possibly down to near the base of the knot will be a very different color from the knot base. Unfortunately there are many exceptions to this rule, which make the eye test fallible.

SMALL-BATCH AND COMMERCIAL DYEING Just as looms vary considerably, so too do the ways of dyeing. A nomadic or village weaver will weave only one rug at a time. She will spin and dye wool herself in a small pot or vat used for this purpose. She will use only one or a few skeins of wool of each color, a method known as small-batch dyeing. By this method, when two or more skeins of a given color are dyed, they usually do not match perfectly in color, so resulting in an effect in the rug called abrash (see below).

In larger rug-weaving enterprises where several looms may be set up in a building and are being used by many weavers, the dyers will calculate the amount of wool needed and use large vats capable of holding a great number of skeins. All of these will be of the same color for the rugs which are about to be woven. This is known as commercial dyeing.

ABRASH is a term associated with dye color in rugs. It refers to a change of tone in a color and shows mainly in the ground color. It occurs when a weaver finishes a

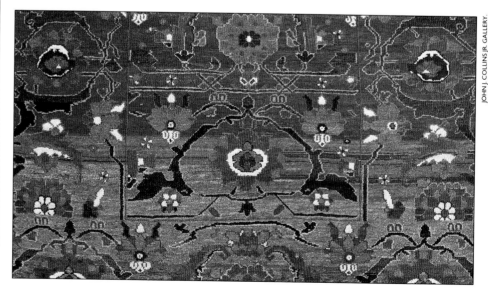

JOHN J. COLLINS JR. GALLERY.

LEFT **This Chahar Mahal carpet c. 1890 is a fine example of abrash shown in the blue field.**

12

PETER PAP ORIENTAL RUGS, INC. PHOTO GARY McKINNIS.

LEFT **This Sarouk mat c. 1930 is typical of the kind of rug that was chemically treated and repainted a deeper blue-red for the U.S. market.**

skein of one color and proceeds using a second skein of the same color but of a slightly different shade. Abrash is usually visible in a straight line across the width of the rug. It is regarded as a positive rather than a negative feature, if the color change is not too sharp or distinct. Abrash is usually the result of small-batch dyeing and indicates that the rug was made by one weaver. It may also result from the use of leftover wool from another rug. It is one of those "imperfections" that handmade Oriental rugs are "supposed" to have.

Although abrash is closely associated with natural dyes, it does not follow that all rugs with abrash were woven with naturally dyed fibres. Abrash is considered a point of beauty and subtlety not only by Westerners but by the weavers as well. Many large carpets made by sophisticated weavers and dyers have abrash deliberately inserted into the design of the carpet.

CHEMICAL TREATMENT OF DYES From the end of the nineteenth century there is evidence of the chemical treatment of rugs to alter their color, a process commonly known as stripping. Stripping is done by washing a rug in a chemical solution to change the color of one or more of its dyes. The rug may be sold in this new stripped color, or one or more of the stripped colors may be painted with a fresh color. A group of rugs from the eastern Caucasus, woven at the end of the century in magenta, gold, blue, and ivory, was stripped: the magenta and gold changed to tones of beige, tan, and off-white, leaving only the blue in its original state.

Another group of rugs, primarily from Sarouk in Persia, was woven in a rust-red in the 1920s and 1930s. This red was not much liked in the United States, so it was chemically washed to change it to pink. The pink was painted a magenta red, which was commercially popular. These rugs are called painted Sarouks.

Throughout most of this century it has been common practice to give new rugs a light chemical wash to soften the newness of the colors. This was done to most room-size carpets and many smaller rugs in London, Hamburg, and New York by the wholesale dealers. It is still done today on certain classes of rug, including many of the new natural-dyed ones. Most collectors avoid rugs that have received this treatment.

RUG TYPES AND SIZES

For the Oriental rug collector the size and use of a weaving is frequently as important as any other feature. Size and use play a role in determining whether a rug is considered commercial or collectible. The term commercial means that a rug was intentionally made for sale, particularly for the Western market. Collectible implies that the rug was made mainly for use by the weaver to satisfy a need of his or her lifestyle. The assumption is that it was not made primarily with a foreign buyer in mind.

Carpets are usually larger than 9 × 6ft. in size. Very few people collect carpets but have them for decorative purposes.

Rugs are usually smaller than 9 × 6ft. Some of these are considered to be commercial and some are

collectible. Rugs from all countries are collected by many people.

Runners usually measure some 3–4ft. wide and 8–20ft. or more in length. Generally they are treated as commercial weavings in view of their specific use.

Prayer rugs are typically 2–4 × 4–8ft. They are one of the more popular types with collectors. A variety of terms for prayer rugs is found in rug literature, including sejadeh, namazlyk, and joi namaz. Some prayer rugs were made for use by more than one person; the term for such rugs is saph.

Donkeybags, about 2 × 4–5ft. in size, are utilitarian weavings for carrying goods. They are one of the most popular types for collectors. Most older donkeybags were cut apart and sold as small rugs, known as bagfaces (in Persian, khorjin).

Juvals are single bags made in many different

Carpet

Donkeybag

Rug

Prayer rug

Runner

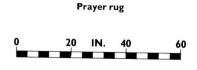

0   20   IN.   40   60

Juval

14

rectangular sizes: 1–3 × 4–7ft. Juvals were typically made in pairs. As with donkeybags, the backs of these were cut off and sold as small rugs. Other terms used for juval-type weavings in other sizes are torba and mafrash.

Other utilitarian weavings were made for specific daily and festive needs. Some of these are tentbands, animal trappings for wedding ceremonies, coverings for animals such as horses and camels, and other specialized functions. These weavings are among some of the most desired by collectors.

Flatweaves are made in all of the above sizes and with the same utilitarian functions. Twenty-five years ago very few Oriental rug collectors paid any attention to these weavings, but today they are avidly collected. With the exception of how they are woven, all of the information given so far about pile rugs applies also to flatweaves; the latter differ in their construction in that they do not have knotted pile, except in certain instances. Flatweaves have a warp and a weft, but the number of techniques employed in their construction is much more varied and diverse than in pile carpets. Identification is by technique, the two most common types being kilim and soumak.

Kilims are the simplest of these constructions. Here the warp is the foundation and the weft is dyed and woven over the warp to create the pattern. In their purest form kilims are reversible and usable on both sides. Kilims are a tapestry weave. The most common techniques are called slitweave and dovetail. Slitweave results in short vertical slits in the kilim and dovetail kilims do not have slits.

Soumaks are more complex and are not reversible. An extra weft of dyed wool is used to create the pattern. These pattern wefts are wrapped around the warps in a regular sequence. They are cut and hang loose on the back of the rug. Soumaks are a brocade weave.

Other flatweave techniques are used to employ different methods of inserting pattern warps and wefts. Among them are cicim, zili, and verneh. They are known as compound weaves.

KILIMS AND SOUMAKS

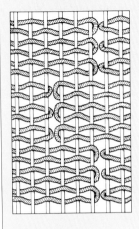 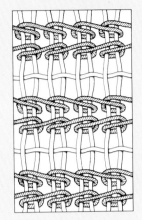

1 Kilim, or slit tapestry weave
2 Soumak brocading with ground weave

Kilim rug showing the slit tapestry weave.

Soumak rug illustrating the brocade weave.

15

THE RUG FORMAT

The terms used to describe the format of a weaving, whether pile or flatweave, donkeybag or juval, are essentially the same. Most rugs are square or rectangular in shape, though there are also round, pentagonal, and U-shaped weavings: again, the same terminology is used for all. The most commonly used English terms are:

Field: The large area in the center of a rug. It is surrounded by the borders and contains the main patterns and designs.

Field color or ground color: The (usually) single color on which the design is arranged.

Pattern: Specific types of elements used to create a design on the field and borders of a rug.

Design: The overall impression created on the field of a rug. Designs are primarily all-over or centred. An all-over design is typically one in which the same pattern is used repetitively on the field. A centered or medallion design is typically one with a medallion around which other secondary patterns are arranged.

Spandrels: Centered designs frequently have quarter-medallions or distinctively different patterns in the corners of the field, these patterns are known as spandrels.

Borders: These may vary from one to ten or more in number and are bands or stripes, usually of varying width, around the perimeter of a rug.

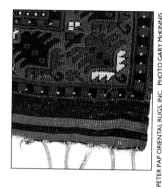

LEFT **Bergama prayer rug, 3ft. 3in. × 3ft.10in., c. 1900. The prayer rugs attributed to the village of Yacibedir commonly have a star-filled, dark blue mihrab and red borders with this leaf form. The red, white, and blue is typical of west Anatolia.**

PETER PAP ORIENTAL RUGS, INC. PHOTO GARY McKINNIS

Ends: The ends are usually the two shortest sides of a rug. They may consist of a flatwoven area, 1in.–1ft. deep. In older, used rugs this is one of the first areas to show wear and may be missing entirely.

Fringe: This extends out from the ends and is the exposed warps. It may be 1–10in. long when new. Like the ends, it wears first and may be very uneven. In some types of rug the fringe may be braided or knotted in unusual ways.

Edge: Usually the two long sides of a rug. They may be finished in one of two ways, called overcast and selvage, to create a durable finish.

An overcast is a group of warps wrapped with a separate thread in a circular fashion; this type of finish has a rounded look. A selvage has pairs of warps covered by a figure-eight wrapping, which creates a flatter, wider edge than overcasting.

Skirt: Some weavings such as juvals and donkeybags have an additional wide border, known as a skirt, on one side of the rug.

PETER PAP ORIENTAL RUGS, INC.

ABOVE **Bergama rug, 3ft. 6in. × 4ft. 10in., c. 1880. The saturated colors of this rug are found in rugs of west and** central Anatolia. Note the knotted Arabic script in the kilim end.

PRIVATE COLLECTION.

ABOVE **Kurdish juval, 2ft. × 3ft. 5in., c. 1900. This kilim from** east Anatolia was originally a bag.

PATTERNS

Patterns used in rugs may vary in shape, size, or drawing, but the basic form remains recognizable.

Most patterns have descriptive names; some of the more common ones are:

Rosette

Leaf

Palmette

Gul

Arabesque, tendril, or vine

Boteh

Herati border

Trefoil

Mina Khani

Medallion

Tree of Life

Mihrab

Rosette: Horizontal cross section of a flower.

Palmette: Vertical cross section of a flower.

Leaf: Flat pattern with a leaf shape.

Arabesque, tendril, or vine: Straight or curved line connecting pattern elements.

Herati: Complex arrangement of rosettes, palmettes, and leaves around a diamond and frequently used in simplified forms.

Mina khani: Complex arrangement of rosettes and palmettes on a vine and frequently used in simplified forms.

Boteh: Elongated figure similar to a leaf but wider and rounder at the bottom. Also called paisley, pine cone, or shawl pattern.

Gul: Polygon with various motifs within it.

Medallion: Large central field pattern used one or more times as the focus for a design.

Trefoil: Three-part pattern on a base used mainly in minor borders.

Tree of Life: Tree shape frequently used on prayer rugs.

Mihrab: Arch-shaped form used on prayer rugs.

THE ELEMENTS OF A PATTERN are embellishments used to enhance its complexity or importance. Some of the more common ones are:

Latchhook: Hooked device generally used around the edge of geometric forms.

Lattice: Series of connected lines that create an openwork structure.

Filler elements: Geometric, floral, and animal forms used to fill spaces between pattern elements.

Lattice

Latchhook

Filler elements

METHODS OF DRAWING PATTERNS vary from country to country according to the type of weaver – that is, nomadic, village, or city. They may be characterized as:

Abstract or geometric: That is, with straight or stepped outlines.

Representational or curvilinear: That is, with curved or rounded outlines.

Persianate: Closely associated with rugs from Iran such as the herati, mina khani, boteh, and arabesque.

THE MEANING OF PATTERNS is one of the most written-about aspects of Oriental rugs and one of the least understood. Scholars have traced the evolution of designs, their origins, and how they have changed over time and under different empires. There are various theories as to the original meanings of some patterns. Most weavers today, however, frequently attach quite different meanings to patterns from those of scholars. Unfortunately space restrictions prevent an examination here of this complex subject.

JOHN J. COLLINS JR. GALLERY.

THE
CLASSIFICATION
OF RUGS
AND CARPETS

CHAPTER 2

Rugs are divided in two principal ways to form discrete groups with similar or like characteristics: according to the lifestyle of the weaver and to the geographic area of the world in which they are made. Although most rug types have sets of distinguishing characteristics, there will always be exceptions to distinctions based on lifestyle and geography. The collector should bear in mind that these are merely guidelines, and not hard-and-fast rules.

THE LIFESTYLE OF THE WEAVER

Lifestyle refers to how the weaver makes a living, what type of dwelling he or she lives in, and for what purpose the weaving was intended. These aspects of the weaver's life are reflected in the size of rugs woven, the patterns used in them, the materials spun for the threads, the choice of dyes and colors, and the technical methods employed in weaving.

The terms used to describe a weaver's lifestyle are nomadic, village, and city. Each rug displays characteristics that are clues to the weaver's lifestyle: these are choice of materials for the warp and weft, number of colors used, edge and end finish, pile height, types of pattern, size and shape of weavings, and other technical features.

Materials: Clues to identification of the weaver's lifestyle lie in whether warp and weft are all wool, all cotton, or a mixture of the two. Cotton usage implies settlement. Sheep that produce wool may be free-roaming, implying nomadism of their keepers, or may be kept in a contained pasturage by settled people.

Number of colors refers to the number of different colors a weaver uses to create the patterns of a rug. Nomads use the fewest and city weavers the most.

ABOVE LEFT **Bijar carpet, 8 × 18ft., c. 1840. This design is a strapwork and lattice arabesque with flowering plants. It is a version of a garden carpet design dating from the seventeenth century. Its size and the reconciled corners of the main border identify it as a workshop carpet.**

Edge and end finish refers to the use of selvage or overcast, whether the sides are even or uneven, the degree to which the widths of the two ends are equal, the depth of the kilim finish on each end, and the length of the fringe. These features reveal the type of loom used by a weaver. Selvages occur most often in nomadic and village rugs and overcast typify city ones.

Pile height is the depth of the pile. In cutting the knot, the weaver wants to leave it long enough so that the knot ends and adjacent knots do not separate, thus exposing the warp and weft threads. Therefore the length of pile is a reflection of the knot density and in general, nomadic rugs have a lower density than city rugs.

Types of pattern covers whether the patterns are geometric or floral and the degree of their angularity. The way a weaver handles the border corners also comes under this heading. Border corners may be described as reconciled or unreconciled, terms that refer to the way the pattern turns the 90-degree angle of the corner. If they are chopped off and abutted, they are known as unreconciled. If the pattern is drawn in an unbroken 45-degree turn, it is known as reconciled. Nomadic rugs are the most geometric, city rugs the most curvilinear. Village rugs are in-between. City and workshop rugs have reconciled corners and nomadic and village rugs are unreconciled.

Sizes and shapes indicates whether the weavings are primarily rugs or whether they include utilitarian weavings such as donkeybags, juvals, and animal trappings. Nomads make utilitarian pieces and village and city weavings are mostly rugs and carpets.

Technical features are the use of warp depression; silk as a thread for warp, weft, or pile; and knot density. These vary with all types of weavers and are specific aspects which a serious collector should learn.

NOMADIC The nomadic lifestyle in its purist form suggests people who live in a portable dwelling, typically a black tent or yurt; who have flocks of sheep, horses, camels, and goats; who move from place to place with some frequency; and who are more or less totally dependent on their animals and the land for their

PRIVATE COLLECTION.

ABOVE **Shahsavan bagface, 1ft. 10in. × 1ft. 10in., c. 1850. The latchhook or "ram's head" motif is used to great effect throughout the border and field patterns of this piece. The light-colored areas of four of the animals and the four birds in the center have silk highlights.**

living. This means weaving on a portable loom, using dye colors that can be obtained from free-growing plants, and weavings that serve the needs of everyday life. Nomadic weavers use a relatively limited pattern and design range, reflecting the cultural traditions of the group. The weaver uses memorized patterns that are repeated and varied from one weaving to the next.

Bearing in mind these facts, it is possible to look for the following characteristics in their rugs:

Materials: The warps and wefts should be all wool.

Number of colors: Few in number, generally from three to seven.

Edge and end finish: The edge will usually be finished with a selvage, sometimes with horsehair or goathair. The edges will be irregular and the ends may differ in width by several inches. The kilim finish may be plain, colored, patterned, or striped and 1–15in. in width. The fringe will be 5–10in. in length and may be braided.

Pile height: Varies from medium to long.

Types of pattern: Geometric. Floral and animate forms are simple and angular. All-over patterns predominate. Border corners are unreconciled.

Sizes and shapes: Numerous.

Technical features: Most nomadic weavers' rugs are

woven with warps on one level – that is, not depressed. Some may show minor depression. The average knot density is below 80 per square inch. Silk is sometimes used in special pieces, but only for a few knots or in small areas.

VILLAGE Weavers who live in agricultural communities are described as having a village lifestyle. Like nomads they may keep sheep, horses, and goats, but the herding and tending of animals is not their main source of livelihood. They grow various crops including cotton, which is available in sufficient quantity for them to spin it and use it in rugs in place of wool. Because they are settled they build permanent looms of the upright type. They may have a wider range of dye materials than nomads.

Village weavers are able to weave for longer periods throughout the year and in some cases year-round. Woven articles are produced for sale as well as for community use, because they have contact with the larger social community, they are exposed to patterns from other villages and towns.

Village rugs have the following characteristics:

Materials: Warps are mostly cotton and wefts may be either wool or cotton.

Number of colors: The range is from five to ten, with a variety of blue shades and distinct greens.

Edge and end finish: The edges are finished in both ways, but overcast edges are more common. The edges are even and there is less difference in the width of the two ends. The kilim on each end is 1–2in. wide and may be natural or a dyed color. The fringe is 1–4in. in length. On many rugs the fringe on one end is not cut but exists as warp loops.

Pile height: Medium to short.

Types of pattern: A broad range of patterns is used, both geometric and floral, but the drawing is angular, not rounded. The designs may be all-over or centred. Border corners are unreconciled.

Sizes and shapes: The sizes vary considerably from 2 × 4ft. to 10 × 18ft. Most of village production is floor rugs in various sizes. There are some utilitarian

weavings such as donkeybags and covers for horses, bedding, and food.

Technical features: Most village rugs are woven with the warps on one level, but many have depressed warps. The knot density is mostly 60–120 knots per square inch. Silk is used only in special pieces and in small quantities.

CITY The city lifestyle exhibits the fullest range of skills needed for the most intricately designed and woven carpets. At the city level, weaving is an established commercial activity and is conducted in workshops where the number of looms may range from a few to scores. The weaving process is divided among a variety of skilled craftspeople: hand and machine spinners, dyers, design artists, loom builders and warpers, weavers, and finally finishers. In contrast to nomadic and village weaving, where the weaver creates the rug from wool to finished product, no one person can be said to have "woven" a city carpet.

The characteristics of city rugs are as follows:

Materials: Warps and wefts are primarily cotton. Wool is used for the pile. Silk may be used for warp, weft, and pile.

Number of colors: Usually from eight to twenty.

Edge and end finish: The edges are primarily finished with an overcast of cotton.

Looms are permanent: The ends are of equal width. The kilim finish may be from a fraction of an inch to more than an inch wide. The fringe is 1–4in. long.

Pile height: Medium to short.

Types of pattern: Mostly curvilinear. The designs are drawn on graph paper by trained artists, so the weavers know how to create the curved lines and reconciled corners. Most patterns have a medallion, arabesques, and spandrels. All-over designs are also used.

Sizes and shapes: Almost all are rugs and carpets.

Technical features: Many rugs are woven with warp depression. Most have more than 100 knots per square inch, though as many as 300–600 are common. Silk is often used.

NORTHAMPTON COLLEGE LIBRARY

THE GEOGRAPHIC APPROACH

The traditional rug-weaving areas are Turkey, the Caucasus, Iran, Central Asia, and China. The rugs of each area have distinctive technical features, of which the most important are described below.

TURKEY The three rug-weaving areas of Turkey are the western, central, and eastern regions. City rugs are woven mostly in the western region, nomadic rugs predominate in the eastern region, while village rugs are woven throughout the country. The major characteristics of Turkish rugs are given below.

Knot type: Symmetric.

Knot density: Coarse to medium, with 40–90 knots per square inch. City rugs have a higher knot density.

Warp and weft fibers: Wool is used for warp and weft in nomadic and most village rugs. Wool wefts are frequently dyed red, but brown and yellow are also

ABOVE **Three-medallion Kazak rug, 5ft. 5in. × 8ft. 6in., c. 1910. In earlier versions of this design a different pattern would have been used for the interior of** the center or two end medallions. The random figures in the field are often used by Caucasian weavers.

used. Cotton is used for warps and wefts in city rugs. Silk is used only in minor details in nomadic and village rugs. Many city rugs may be all silk or silk may be used only for the pile.

Dyes and colors: All colors are used. The presence of certain colors sets Turkish rugs apart: purples, yellows, oranges, greens, and salmons. A blue-red dye from cochineal often appears. The browns are mostly corrosive.

Rug sizes: All sizes are made, but the most common are small rugs ranging in overall dimensions from 2 × 4ft. to 6 × 9ft. There are many types of prayer rugs and villagers and nomads produce a wide variety of types of bags.

ABOVE **Konya prayer rug, 4ft. 9in. × 5ft.7in., c. 1850. The architectural prayer arch supported by columns derives from seventeenth-century** Turkish rugs. This village weaver used patterns including a water ewer, a symbol of cleanliness often found on prayer rugs.

PETER PAP ORIENTAL RUGS, INC.   PHOTO GARY McKINNIS.

PETER PAP ORIENTAL RUGS, INC.   PHOTO GARY McKINNIS.

Types of pattern and design: A full range of patterns is used. Geometric and angular floral patterns predominate in both centered and all-over designs.

Technical features: Edge finishes are mostly selvage. Fringes may be long or short and with narrow or 4–7-in. wide kilims. Pile height is varied. Warp depression occurs mostly in city rugs.

THE CAUCASUS Caucasian rugs are mostly village rugs, though a group of large carpets was woven in cities. The major characteristics of Caucasian rugs are given below.

Knot type: Symmetric.

Knot density: Coarse to fine, most rugs being 40–120 knots per square inch.

Warp and weft fibers: Wool is used predominantly for warp and weft. Wefts are natural and dyed red, blue, and yellow. In some areas cotton is used too.

Dyes and colors: Primary colors – red, blue, and yellow – are common as well as green, orange, and purple. A corrosive brown is used.

Rug sizes: Most are from 2 × 4ft. to 6 × 8ft. Large city rugs are two and a half times long as wide. Many donkeybags are made.

Types of design and pattern: Patterns are geometric and angular. Two or three large medallions and all-over designs are common. Small filler elements are scattered on the field. Prayer rugs are common. Border corners are unreconciled. City rugs have Persianate patterns.

Technical features: Edge finishes are selvage and overcast. Fringes are 3–7in. or braided. Kilim ends are not more than 2–4in. wide. Pile height varies.

IRAN OR PERSIA Iranian or Persian rugs are woven in all areas of the country and cover the entire range of nomadic, village, and city weaving. The major characteristics of Iranian rugs are given below.

Knot type: Symmetric and asymmetric.

Knot density: Coarse to fine, 30–1,000 knots or more per square inch.

Warp and weft fibers: Wool, cotton, and silk are used.

Dyes and colors: The entire spectrum is used.

Sizes of rug: All sizes and shapes are produced.

Types of design and pattern: All types of patterns and designs are used.

Technical features: All types of edge finishes, warp and weft fibers and fringes are found. Kilim ends may be 1–6in. wide. Pile length varies.

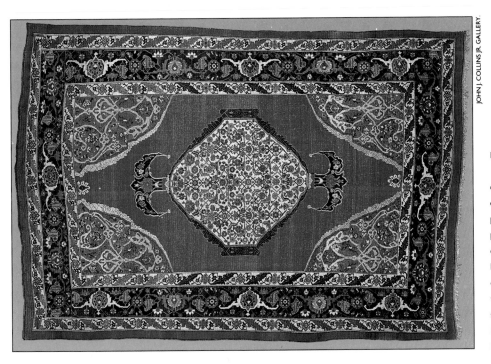

JOHN J. COLLINS JR. GALLERY.

LEFT **Bijar carpet, 9ft. 6in. × 14ft., c. 1870. This is the quintessential Bijar carpet: open red field, large, herati-pattern medallion with pendant anchors, contrasting color spandrels and a few wide borders. The main border exhibits the border version of the herati pattern. The secondary border of "oak" leaves and rosettes is virtually Bijar property.**

CENTRAL ASIAN AND TURKOMAN (KAZAKHSTAN, UZBEKISTAN, TURKMENISTAN, KYRGYZSTAN AND TAJIKISTAN) RUGS are mostly nomadic and village rugs. The major characteristics of these rugs are given below.

Knot type: Symmetric and asymmetric.

Knot density: Coarse to fine, 30–200 knots per square inch.

Warp and weft fibers: Wool is used for both. Wefts are mostly brown wool.

Dyes and colors: Reds varying from reddish-brown to purple predominate. Secondary colors are blue, blue-green, white, brown, and yellow.

Rug sizes: All sizes and shapes are produced.

Types of design and pattern: Patterns are geometric and all-over designs. Border corners are unreconciled.

Technical features: Edge finishes are mostly selvage. Kilim ends may be 2–15in. in width. Fringes are 6–10in. long. Pile depth varies.

CHINA Chinese rugs are mostly woven in north China, Tibet, and Xinjiang, primarily in urban centers. Their major characteristics are given below.

Knot type: Asymmetric, except in Tibet where a looping technique is used.

Knot density: Medium to coarse, 40–80 knots per square inch.

Warp and weft fibers: Cotton predominates, but wool was used for wefts in older Xinjiang and Tibetan rugs.

Dyes and colors: Colors differ in each area.

Rug sizes: Large sizes predominate among Chinese rugs, small ones among Tibetan and medium-sized ones among Xinjiang.

Types of design and pattern: Traditional Chinese patterns in centered and all-over designs. Border corners are reconciled except in Xinjiang rugs.

Technical features: Edge finishes in Chinese rugs are overcast in cotton. Selvages are used in Xinjiang. Fringes are 2–5in. Kilim ends are usually not more than 1–4in. wide. The pile depth is thick except in some Xinjiang rugs.

Neither of these two approaches to rug classification

should be used without reference to the other. They complement each other and assist not only in the identification of rugs but in their appreciation as well. When considering the lifestyle of the weaver, you are concentrating more on why a particular rug may have been made, its use, and the source of the materials. The geographic approach provides a broader view of the social, cultural, and political context in which a rug was woven, how the aesthetics of, say, a Safavid or an Ottoman court influenced the weaver and how that culture shows in the rug.

PETER PAP ORIENTAL RUGS, INC. PHOTO GARY McKINNIS.

ABOVE **Chinese seat cover, 2ft. 2in. × 2ft. 2in., c. 1880. The coloration of this rug is usually associated with Ning Hsia, one of the principal weaving centers of China. The border pattern is called mountains and waves.**

RIGHT **Uzbek mafrash, 1ft. × 3ft. 6in., c. 1880. Long, narrow pieces like this were mostly made into bags to hold bed linen. They served a variety of purposes in the Uzbek yurt. The patterning of the end panels of this piece are especially dramatic and different.**

DENNIS AND MAILE MARQUAND. PHOTO GARY McKINNIS.

GEORGE FINE KILIMS.

THE RUGS OF ANATOLIA/ TURKEY

CHAPTER 3

The rugs of Anatolia have been known in the West longer than any other type and they appear in the earliest paintings. Because Turkish rug patterns and colors are more complex and difficult to appreciate than those belonging to other groups, they are the ones that many collectors learn to appreciate last.

▮ *Types of weaving:* The majority of Turkish rugs are village rugs. Many patterns and designs are associated with specific villages. They were used by the weavers, donated to mosques, and sold in the marketplace.

The city rugs of Turkey are made primarily in and around Istanbul and the cities of Sivas, Izmir, Isparta, and Keyseri. These rugs are almost entirely commercially produced and are of little interest to collectors. Silk rugs are woven in the Istanbul area, the best known and among the finest of their kind being the Herekes.

Nomadic rugs are woven throughout the country, but the greatest numbers come from the eastern region of Turkey. In Turkey nomads are known as *yörüks*, which is also used as a general term for nomadic rugs.

▮ *Sizes:* These vary but most items are rug size: that is, smaller than 6 × 9ft., a reflection of their village and nomadic origin. Carpets are woven primarily in the city workshops. There are large numbers of bags in many different shapes and sizes.

▮ *Patterns:* Geometric and floral patterns are frequently combined. Many floral forms have become almost unrecognizable because of the angular drawing. In fine silk rugs, Persianate, floral, and arabesque patterns dominate.

▮ *Colors:* Mainly primary colors are used (red, blue, yellow) and their combinations (green, orange, purple). The amount of yellow used is much higher than in other rug-weaving areas. Browns are used for outlining and major design areas.

ABOVE LEFT **Ordu Kurdish kilim, 4. × 5ft., c. 1880. The patterns used in this striped kilim are common features in Kurdish weaving. The pattern on the middle, white stripe is called elibilinde (hands on hips). Note the fringe braided into a flat band on each end.**

PRIVATE COLLECTION.

PETER PAP ORIENTAL RUGS, INC.

Synthetic dyes have been used almost from the moment they were discovered. By the early twentieth century these dyes were in use everywhere. Turkish rugs became synonymous with bleeding and fading dyes. The most common colors of this type are bright, bleeding reds, faded purples, and harsh, unfading oranges. Chrome dyes replaced many of these in the 1950s and more recently natural dyes have enjoyed a rebirth in Turkish rug weaving.

Technical characteristics: Many characteristics, such as the symmetric knot, are shared throughout Anatolia. The following table illustrates the ways in which they differ by region, though it should be remembered that there are always exceptions.

ABOVE LEFT Melas rug, 3ft. 7in. × 5ft. 7in., c. 1870. Rugs with stripe patterns are woven in most areas. This Turkish weaver used patterns normally reserved for borders.

ABOVE Melas rug, 3ft. 10in. × 5ft. 10in., c. 1870. The pattern of a flowering plant on the red field is not typical of Melas rugs. However, the colors, pattern of the main border, and flatwoven ends are standard features.

	WEST	CENTRAL	EAST
Warp material color	Wool, white	Wool, mostly white, some brown, mixed	Wool and goathair, white and brown, mixed
Weft material color	Wool, red, some brown and white	Wool, brown, white, red, yellow	Wool mostly brown, blue
Number of Wefts	2–4 or more	2–4 or more	2–4 or more
Warp depression	No depression	Occasional depression	No depression
Edge finish	Selvage, most red and some multicolors	Selvage, red, yellow, and multicolors	Selvage, multicolors "zipper" weave
End finish	Wide red or striped multicolors	Wide red, yellow, or striped multicolors	Wide brown or red, blue, striped colors
Special features	Cochineal red	No cochineal red	Cochineal red; braided fringe

PETER PAP ORIENTAL RUGS, INC.

ABOVE **Mucur prayer rug, 3ft. 6in. × 5ft. 10in., c. 1850.** The shape of the mihrab arch and colors are typical of Mucur prayer rugs. The yellow medallion in the spandrel above it is typical of Kirsheshir, another weaving village in the region. Compare the color use of the main border pattern to the rug on page 16.

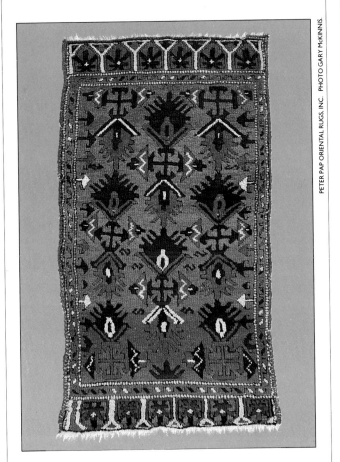

PETER PAP ORIENTAL RUGS, INC.   PHOTO GARY McKINNIS.

ABOVE **Konya yastik, 1ft. 9in. × 3ft. 2in., c. 1870.** Yastiks were made as pillows and used when sitting. The backs have usually been cut off, leaving only the pile face as a small rug. The small lappets at each end are frequently found on them.

BELOW RIGHT **Yoruk rug, 3ft. 8in. × 7ft. 2in., c. 1900.** The many shades of blue, madder, and cochineal, and orange are typical of east Anatolian Yoruk rugs. The brocaded ends and zipperlike selvage are typical as well.

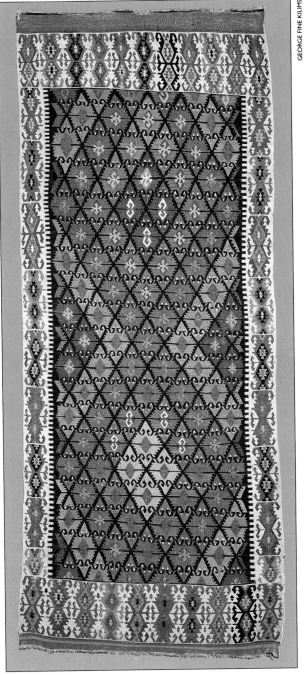

GEORGE FINE KILIMS.

ABOVE **Sivrihisar kilim, 5ft. × 12ft. 9in., c. 1875.** This kilim was woven in one piece with a small repeating pattern used in kilims and pile rugs. In color use and design balance it is a *tour de force* expression of this pattern.

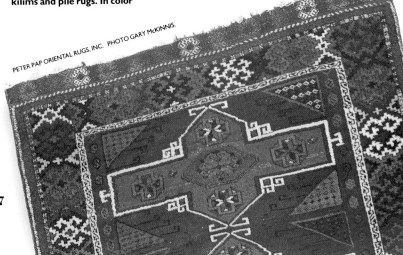

PETER PAP ORIENTAL RUGS, INC.   PHOTO GARY McKINNIS.

27

GEORGE FINE KILIMS.

GEORGE FINE KILIMS.

ABOVE **Konya kilim, 2ft. 10in. × 13ft. 4in., c. 1825.** Many Turkish kilims were woven in two panels which were then sewn together to create a large rug. This is half of such a kilim. The range and intensity of color are typical of early pieces.

ABOVE RIGHT **Obruk prayer kilim, 4ft. 2in. × 5ft. 7in., dated 1892.** The colors, patterns, and design are typical of Obruk village. The date is woven just below the mihrab peak. Note the different end finishes, one a long braided fringe and the other flat.

RUGS OF WESTERN ANATOLIA

If any color scheme predominates in western Anatolia, it is red, white, and blue. This is especially typical for the area between Çanakkale and Bergama. As you proceed south toward Melas, yellow increases in frequency.

Many of the classical rugs from the Ottoman period (1359–1922) that reached the West were woven in this region. The patterns of the so-called Holbein rugs occur in many of the rugs from the Çanakkale-Bergama area. They feature large medallions seen in large-patterned Holbeins or a complex interlocking geometric pattern observed in small-patterned Holbein rugs. Many of the border patterns used are seen in classical Ushak and Transylvanian rugs.

Some western Anatolian rugs prized by collectors sixty to eighty years ago, such as Ghiordes, Kula, and Melas, originate from this region.

RUGS OF CENTRAL ANATOLIA

Today the rugs of central Anatolia are of great interest to collectors. As regards pattern, many are considered successors to the earliest Anatolian rugs. Konya rugs in particular have a high incidence of these patterns. Their coloring includes a generous use of yellow, but rarely cochineal red. Of all Turkish rugs these are the most dramatically colored.

Ladik and Muçur rugs are still prized today, the distinctive prayer rugs being the most widely known. Ladiks are among the most finely woven village rugs; Muçur prayer rugs are simpler and less floral in patterning. Both have simple, stepped mihrabs (arches) with open fields.

Other village names from this region are Taspinar, Yahyali, Maden, and Kirshehir. Central Anatolian rugs commonly have corrosive browns. Many central Anatolian rugs are long runners.

RUGS OF EASTERN ANATOLIA

The rugs of eastern Anatolia are produced mainly by Kurds and nomadic groups referred to as *yörüks*. The patterns are almost entirely geometric, and the edges and ends of the rugs can be very irregular. Two common distinctive and identifying features of rugs from this region are the use of camelhair and a unique selvage that resembles a zipper.

Many designs in large medallion format are found in these rugs. Because they were woven for use in the coldest region of Turkey, the pile was left long for insulation and comfort, although the weave can also be quite fine.

TURKISH FLATWEAVES

Flatweaves were made in all parts of Turkey by both village and nomadic weavers. The entire range of flatweave techniques is found in Turkish weaving, and the patterns and designs employed are the most extensive of any country.

GEORGE FINE KILIMS.

ABOVE **Sivas area kilim, 3ft. 4in. × 5ft., c. 1880. The six-pointed stars depicted in the borders and field of this small kilim are used throughout Turkey. It is uncertain whether** this interesting piece is a **prayer rug because of the apparent mihrab on one end – or did the weaver miscalculate the space needed to finish the red medallion?**

Turkish flatweaves are currently the most popular with collectors and extremely old examples are considered to be among the finest expression of the weaver's art; twenty years ago, however, no one was collecting them. This phenomenal reversal is the result of a realization that flatweaves, more than any other weaving from Turkey, fit today's criteria for collecting: that is, they were made for the weaver's use, not made for commercial purposes, and are derivative of the oldest patterns used in weaving. They are categorized by region in much the same way as are pile rugs, except that there is much more variety in the functional uses for which they were made.

JOHN J. COLLINS JR. GALLERY.

The rugs of the Caucasus are essentially village rugs, and their bold colors, geometric designs, and folk art features appeal to most people. They are easily divided according to design and weave characteristics into those from the western and those from the eastern Caucasus. This division is generally between rugs with large patterns and relatively coarse weave, and those with small patterns and fine weave.

▌*Types of weaving:* As village rugs, most are small to area size and not larger than 6 × 9ft. There are many prayer rugs about 3 × 5ft. Utilitarian pieces are mostly donkeybags and covers. Large rugs were made in workshops in a few cities. Many runners were woven.

▌*Size:* Most items are rug size: that is, smaller than 6 × 9ft., a reflection of their village origin. Many prayer rugs were woven. Carpets were woven in city workshops.

THE RUGS OF THE CAUCASUS

CHAPTER 4

PETER PAP ORIENTAL RUGS, INC

ABOVE LEFT Lori Pambak Kazak rug, 6. × 9ft., c. 1880. This kind of Kazak exemplifies the bold design for which they are noted. The absence of small filler patterns is unusual in this rug type.

ABOVE **Shirvan rug, 122 × 152cm (4 × 5ft), c. 1880. The field and main border contain versions of the mina khani pattern. In the field between two types of rosette a single white flower from this pattern is used as a secondary device.**

PRIVATE COLLECTION.

▌ *Patterns:* Both geometric and floral patterns are used. In the western area, large geometric medallions predominate. In the eastern area smaller patterns are typical.

▌ *Colors:* Red, blue, yellow, green, and white in pure tones are standard.

▌ *Technical characteristics:* The following table illustrates the differences between rugs of the western and eastern areas:

	WESTERN	EASTERN
Type of knot	Symmetric	Symmetric
Density of weave	40–100 knots per square inch	80–200 knots per square inch
Pile height	Medium to high	Short to medium
Warp material color	Wool, white, and mixed brown	Wool, white, few mixed
Weft material color	Wool, natural, and dyed	Wool and cotton, natural
Number of wefts	3 or more	2 rarely more
Edge finish	Wool selvage, some dyed	Some blue wool, some cotton

In both areas the fringe may be long or short. Prayer rugs from both areas are about the same size.

RUGS OF THE WESTERN CAUCASUS

Rugs of the western Caucasus have a reputation for bold patterns, vivid color, and strong designs. The western area is divided into two regions. The rugs from the north are Kazaks; those from the south Karabaghs.

KAZAK RUGS Kazak rugs are among the largest woven. They have a long pile and are made of lustrous wool. The wefts are frequently dyed red and the selvages may be woven in more than one color. Some of the better-known designs are:

Star Kazak: Large eight-pointed stars alternate with eight-pointed medallions. The ground color is white.

Pinwheel Kazak: Typically a red ground with pinwheel medallions in blue with a distinctive secondary pattern in green and white rosettes.

ABOVE **Karachov Kazak rug, 4ft. 8in. × 6ft. 5in., c. 1890.** This is the most common of the Karachov designs. A green field is often used. This rug is smaller and more rectangular than most of the type.

BELOW **Kazak rug, 4ft. 2in. × 5ft. 10in., c. 1880.** The colors and simplicity of patterns used are characteristic of Kazak rugs.

PETER PAP ORIENTAL RUGS, INC.

Karachov Kazak: One large octagon medallion with checkerboard corners and four small square medallions in each corner of the field. Squarish in size.

Shield or Sevan Kazak: The largest medallion which fills the field. There are three variations of the medallion form.

Lori Pambak: One large octagonal medallion with pendant irregular medallions or three large medallions of the same type in different colors.

Three-medallion Kazak: One octagon medallion and two stepped medallions on a red field. The two medallion types are in different colors.

Fachralo Kazak: A large six- or ten-sided medallion containing a smaller medallion in a different color. Small and large sizes.

Borchalu Kazak: Wide main borders with latchhook patterns and a narrow field with small latchhook medallions.

KARABAGH RUGS Karabagh rugs are not as large as Kazaks and are more rectangular in shape. They may have dyed wefts, but dark brown is typical. The dark weft is used for the kilim ends. The pile is shorter than in Kazaks. A typical border is the crab border. Some of the better-known designs are:

Sunburst, Cheleberd, or Eagle Kazak: A large-rayed medallion with a cruciform center. One, two, or three medallions may be used.

ABOVE **Kazak or Karabagh rug, 4ft. 10in. × 7ft. 2in., c. 1900. The colors, border patterns, and medallion shape are typical** of Karabagh rugs. The red wefts are typical of Kazaks. Technical factors do not always ease identification.

Cloudband or Kondzoresk: Octagonal medallions with four pairs of S-shapes in the center. One, two, or three medallions may be used.

Serrate-edge Medallion: Several diamond-shaped medallions closely placed on a field. Frequently made in runner format.

Genje: A term used for rugs with diagonal stripes in different colors. The stripes have botehs or flowers on them.

Shusha and Yerevan: These are city rugs. Most patterns are floral and Persianate. A cochineal red is frequently used. Most have cotton wefts and closely clipped pile. They are the largest of Caucasian rugs; the length is at least two and a half times the width.

Lampa Karabagh: A series of large and small connected medallions with large birds in the field.

RUGS OF THE EASTERN CAUCASUS

Rugs of the eastern Caucasus have strong colors and are finely woven, with many small intricate repeat patterns. This area is divided into three regions. Rugs from the northern section are known as Kubas; south of it the rugs are called Shirvan; the region south of the city of Baku produces rugs with several different qualities and characteristics. The prayer rugs of the eastern Caucasus are particularly finely knotted weavings.

BELOW **Shield Kazak rug, 5ft. 5in. × 7ft. 2in., c. 1880. Of the variations on the shield design,** this is the most elegant. The main border pattern is frequently found on shield, Karachov, and Fachralo Kazak rugs.

PETER PAP ORIENTAL RUGS, INC. PHOTO GARY McKINNIS.

BELOW **Fachralo Kazak prayer rug, 3ft. 9in. × 5ft. 6in., c. 1880.** The mihrab arch is a simple, five-sided band extending between the borders. The main border is dramatic and a superb drawing of the leaf and calyx pattern.

RIGHT **Serrate medallion Karabagh, 5ft. 2in. × 8ft. 3in., c. 1900.** There are many variations on the outline of the medallions of these rugs. However, the visual effect is much the same in all of them. This type was made primarily by Armenian weavers.

PETER PAP ORIENTAL RUGS, INC.

Alpan: This design is similar to Star Kazak but rendered smaller. Alpan rugs frequently exhibit very intense yellows. They are small rugs or runners.

Flower or Snowflake: A medium-sized rosette arranged in diagonally colored rows.

Flower Lattice. An all-over lattice pattern with flowers within the lozenge spaces.

KUBA RUGS Kuba rugs exhibit a great variety of patterns. They have wool wefts and typically more than 100 knots per square inch. Many have blue wool selvage and blue soumak weaving on the ends. They have a higher pile than Shirvan rugs. Many shades of blue and salmon-red are used. Several of the better-known designs are:

Chichi: A pattern of geometric forms in rows including the Memling gul. The main border is distinctive. They have an overall greenish colouration.

Perepedil: A series of "ram's horn" patterns in the center and edge of the field.

Seishour or St. Andrew's Cross: A large cross design repeated one or more times in the field. White and blue fields are common. The main border is a blue-and-white pattern called the Georgian border. Rugs with realistically drawn roses are also called Seishour.

PETER PAP ORIENTAL RUGS, INC.

ABOVE **Shirvan prayer rug, 3ft. 6in. × 4ft. 6in., c. 1860.** All of the patterns in this piece are typical of east Caucasian rugs. Note that the diagonal stripes do not match after being cut by the mihrab. A date is woven on the right at the top of the mihrab.

PETER PAP ORIENTAL RUGS, INC.

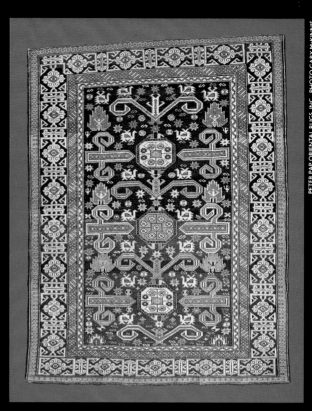

PETER PAP ORIENTAL RUGS, INC.   PHOTO GARY McKINNIS.

PETER PAP ORIENTAL RUGS, INC.

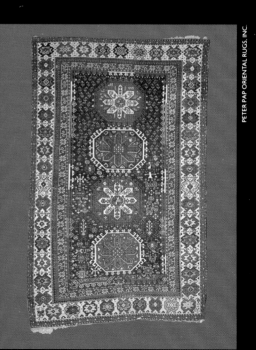

PETER PAP ORIENTAL RUGS, INC.

ABOVE **Chichi prayer rug, 4ft. × 5ft. 2in., c. 1880.** This is the standard version of a Chichi prayer rug. The main border pattern is called the Chichi border. Like many of this type, the rug is dated in the upper right corner of the field.

RIGHT **Kazak rug, 4ft. 3in. × 9ft. 2in., c. 1890.** The series of connected medallions on this rug are frequently found in small Kazak prayer rugs. The slight difference in the size of the medallions enlivens what could be a dull, repetitive pattern.

ABOVE **Perepedil Kuba rug, 3 × 4ft., c. 1880.** The large "ram's horn" patterns in the field are identifiers of Perepedils. The border patterns are found on many types of Kuba rugs.

Except for indigo, this rug was dyed with early synthetic dyes. They faded to pale colors or were chemically treated. See Chapter 1, page 11.

PETER PAP ORIENTAL RUGS, INC.

LEFT **Chichi Shirvan rug, 3ft. 10in. × 5ft. 10in., c. 1880. The patterns used in the field are typical of rugs called Chichi. The Kufic script border pattern is not typical of Chichi rugs, but is common to Shirvan and Kuba rugs.**

BELOW **Seichour Kuba runner, 3ft. 2in. × 11ft., c. 1880. The four large cross designs in the field, the pink floral meander pattern on dark red of the inner border, and the white and blue outer border define the Seichour type rugs.**

PETER PAP ORIENTAL RUGS, INC.
PRIVATE COLLECTION

RIGHT **Chichi rug, 3ft. 9in. × 6ft. 2in., c. 1880. In field and border patterns this is the ideal design for a Chichi rug. It also has the overlying green cast which aesthetically superior examples possess.**

LEFT **Kuba rug, 3ft. 9in. × 6ft., c. 1880. The medallions of this piece have antecedents in sixteenth-century Turkish rugs and persist in Turkoman rugs as the Salor gul. Note that on the beginning end of the rug, the weaver intended to weave two rows of guls but stopped because there was not enough room. This type of change, usually less dramatic, is frequently noted in village and nomadic rugs.**

PETER PAP ORIENTAL RUGS, INC.

GEORGE FINE KILIMS.

ABOVE **Shirvan rug, 3ft. × 5ft. 6in., c. 1880.** This rug includes, in its design, patterns from many different types of rug common to the Caucasus. Not all designs have specific names. The main border pattern is the most common form of the leaf and calyx pattern.

BELOW **Shirvan rug, 3ft. 10in. × 5ft. 10in., c. 1880.** Although frequently used in Shirvan rugs, the Lesghi Star, as the three large stellate medallions are known, is found in most rugs of the Caucasus.

PRIVATE COLLECTION.

ABOVE **Talish kilim, 5ft. × 10ft. 5in., c. 1880.** The design of this kilim is composed of horizontal rows of two types of diamonds. One type has straight edges and the other dentate edges. This creates an ambiguity between where one diamond ends and another starts.

BELOW **Shirvan prayer rug, 3ft. 4in. × 4ft. 9in., c. 1880.** This is the prototypical Shirvan prayer rug in every respect. There is more variety in the flowers within the lattice than is often the case. The white cotton kilim used in the Shirvan region is quite visible.

PETER PAP ORIENTAL RUGS, INC. PHOTO GARY McKINNIS.

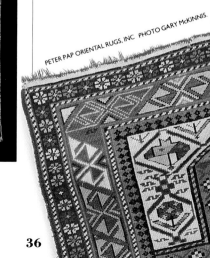

SHIRVAN RUGS Shirvan rugs share many patterns with Kubas, but they differ technically. They have cotton wefts and overcast edges, which may be cotton or wool. The pile is clipped short. Several of the better-known designs are:

Lesghi Star: A large, geometric, eight-pointed star with stepped edges. Several may be used on the field.

Boteh: This pattern was woven in many variations in both rugs and prayer rugs. Color usage can be quite original.

Garden: A series of linked rectangles and octagons, giving the impression of the layout of a Persian garden.

Bijov: A complex group of interlocking palmette and bracket patterns in an ascending arrangement. Blues, pinks, salmons, yellow, and ivory are colors that are commonly featured.

Akstafa: Several large eight-pointed medallions alternating with large birds. The main border is usually white with large geometric patterns. The warp and weft material of these rugs is quite varied.

BAKU, TALISH, LENKORAN, AND MOGHAN RUGS

These come from south of Baku. For organizational purposes they are considered as originating from a single geographic region, though they differ structurally.

Baku: The standard design has an ivory central medallion on a blue field filled with botehs. The main border is ivory or pale blue with alternating rosettes and birds. They are city rugs, though village versions of the same design were made.

Talish: These are wide runners with plain, unpatterned, mostly blue fields. The main border is white, with an alternating pattern of one large and four small rosettes. They have wool warps and cotton or wool wefts.

Lenkoran: These are structurally similar to Talish, but they are more coarsely woven and have a distinctive medallion.

Moghan: The Memling gul and a latchhook diamond are the most common pattern. Many have cotton warps and wefts of a heavy quality.

PETER PAP ORIENTAL RUGS, INC.

ABOVE Bijov Kuba rug, 2ft. 7in. × 4ft., c. 1870. Although small for a Caucasian rug, this is a superb example in color, drawing, and design of the Bijov pattern. The single border does not compete with or detract from the complex forms and arrangement of the field. Note the blue selvage, typical of Kuba rugs.

GEORGE FINE KILIMS.

ABOVE Kuba kelim, 4ft. 7in. × 8ft. 2in., c. 1825. East Caucasian kilims with this design are often called Kuba. The medallions are large and spaciously arranged diagonally by color. These features, coupled with the very simple main border, account for its early dating.

37

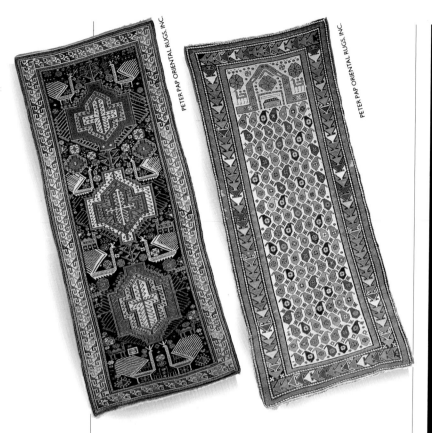

PETER PAP ORIENTAL RUGS, INC.

PETER PAP ORIENTAL RUGS, INC. PHOTO GARY McKINNIS.

ABOVE **Akstafa rug, 4ft. 6in. ×
9ft. 6in., c. 1880. Rugs with
large, peacock-like birds
alternating with medallions are
known as Akstafa. Their
technical characteristics are
varied, and this rug exhibits
features of Kuba.**

ABOVE **Akstafa prayer rug,
2ft. 10in. × 6ft., c. 1880. Akstafa
prayer rugs do not have
peacocks. They are longer in
relation to width than other
prayer rugs. The mihrab arch
with a comb beneath and two
animal figures beside it is
frequently seen in them.**

ABOVE **Kuba soumak carpet,
6ft. 11in. × 8ft. 10in. c. 1890.
Three medallions of this type
form the most common design
used in soumak carpets from
the Caucasus. The filler**

**patterns of the field and
borders vary. The sixteen-
pointed star in the center of
the medallion, for example, is
not common.**

CAUCASIAN FLATWEAVES

Caucasian flatweaves possess many of the same
characteristics of color and design as the rugs. They
were woven primarily for use by the weaver as rugs,
curtains, room dividers, wrappers, and covers, and for
agricultural purposes. They have been attributed to
areas such as Kuba and Shirvan, but they are more
easily organized by weave structure. The main types
are:

Kilims: The two main designs are wide and narrow
horizontal bands with geometric patterns or large
palmettes arranged in diagonally colored rows. Both are
about 5–7 × 8–11ft.

Soumaks: These are large and have a wider design
range than kilims. Two of the most common designs are
the dragon and three medallion types. Donkeybags,
bedding bags, saltbags, and other utilitarian items were
made using this technique.

Zilis: The most common pattern is an S-shaped
dragon. Most zilis were woven in two pieces and sewn
together to create a rug with measurements of 6–7 ×
10–11ft.

Vernehs: The patterns are more varied and smaller in
size, typically made in one piece. Many horsecovers
and hangings were produced using this technique.

Cicims: These have large squares as patterns and are
used in bedding bags, hangings, and donkeybags.

PRIVATE COLLECTION.

THE RUGS OF IRAN

CHAPTER 5

I ranian rugs cover the entire range of types more comprehensively than those of any other country. For centuries village and city weaving in Iran has been of a commercial nature, though most of the country's nomadic and tribal rugs were unaffected by this. To understand Iranian rugs it is best to consider them from the point of view of the weaver's lifestyle.

TRIBAL AND NOMADIC RUGS

Tribal and nomadic rugs are produced by several ethnic groups. They include the Kurds, Bakhtiari and Luri, Qashqai and Khamseh, Afshar, Baluchi, and Shahsavan. Some of these groups are both settled and nomadic.

KURDISH RUGS Kurds inhabit Turkey, Iran, Iraq, and Syria. They weave rugs in all these countries, but in Iran they are a major weaving group. The Kurds are found in the west from the Turkish border in the north, then southward along the Iraqi border and into central Iran. Another group is located in the north east.

Kurdish rugs use a wide range of patterns, types, and styles. The Kurds are master colorists, and their rugs exhibit possibly the finest carpet wools, overall, of those of any nomadic tribes. Kurdish wool is durable, lustrous, and highly receptive to dyes. The general technical characteristics of Kurdish rugs are:

Knot type: Symmetric.

Warp and weft fibers: Mostly wool, with some use of cotton. Warps are mostly white wool, but may be mixed with brown. Wefts are mostly brown; some are red.

Edge finish: Selvage and overcast.

End finish: A wide variety from only 1in. to wide kilims with stripes.

ABOVE LEFT **Malayer prayer rug, 4ft. 7in. × 6ft. 3in., c. 1860.** Few village prayer rugs equal city rugs in sophistication of design, color complexity, and design originality. This one surpasses most of them on all these levels. The wide single main border in yellow is unique. The cypress tree, composed of the herati border pattern is reconciled perfectly, and the color balance is ideal.

PETER PAP ORIENTAL RUGS, INC.

ABOVE **Kurdish rug, 4ft. 3in. ×
7ft. 3in., c. 1850. Kurdish rugs
show infinite pattern and
design variety. This one has a**
**version of the avshan pattern.
Gold and yellow are frequently
the major colors in Kurdish
rugs.**

Dyes and colors: Yellow is a significant color. Both
natural and corrosive browns were used.

A group of weavings, mostly bagfaces, were made by
Jaf Kurds. The main design is a simple latchhook
medallion repeated many times in a lattice. They are
identified by the use of offset knots.

The *Kuchan Kurds* of northeastern Iran produce
rugs, bags, and a variety of utilitarian weavings. Their
patterns are mostly geometric in both all-over and
medallion designs.

Kurdish village rugs are primarily identified with
Hamadan, Senneh, and Bijar. Hamadan is one of the
largest commercial weaving areas, but its rugs are not
collected. The rugs of Senneh and Bijar (to the north of
Senneh) are also commercial but are collected. They
have characteristics that distinguish them from all other
rugs.

Sennehs are among the finest woven village rugs
from west-central Iran. They are single-wefted, with a
very short pile and no warp depression. The back of a
Senneh rug feels like fine sandpaper – its
distinguishing characteristic. When a Senneh rug is not
as finely woven as expected, it is called a Senneh Kurd.

PETER PAP ORIENTAL RUGS, INC.   PHOTO GARY McKINNIS.

ABOVE **Baluchi rug, 3ft. 6in. ×
8ft. 7in., c. 1920. Baluchi rugs
exhibit a wide variety of
patterns and palettes. This is
one of the most typical: brick
reds, brown, and dark blues in
repeating geometric designs.
The white minor borders are a
signature feature.**

BELOW **Jaf Kurd bagface, 2ft.
4in. × 2ft. 3in., c. 1920. The
design and colours are typical
of Jaf Kurd weavings. They are
identified by offset knotting.
The ends were often finished
with brocaded patterns as at
the bottom of this piece. The
top is dovetail and slit tapestry
weave.**

PETER PAP ORIENTAL RUGS, INC.   PHOTO GARY McKINNIS.

PETER PAP ORIENTAL RUGS, INC. PHOTO GARY McKINNIS.

Bijars are among the sturdiest rugs woven. They have depressed warps and are very compact. Most Bijars are carpets, but there are some small rugs and bags. They have great design and pattern variety. Those of lesser quality are referred to as Bijar Kurd.

Veramin, a town south of Tehran, is noted for a particular group of nomadic weavings. Most of them are bagfaces with blue fields and Turkoman guls. The colors are clear and the wool lustrous.

JOHN J. COLLINS JR. GALLERY.

ABOVE **Bijar Kurd rug, 4ft. 2in. × 6ft. 7in., c. 1890. Rugs which exhibit some Bijar and Senneh characteristics but not strongly enough to be called by those names, have Kurd added as an attribution. As with this rug, the patterns are simpler and the color usage more tribal.**

RIGHT **Veramin bagface, 1ft. 8in. × 2ft., c. 1900. Veramin weavings, almost all of which are from bags, display the deeply saturated reds and blue of this piece. The wools are soft and lustrous, and the designs are frequently simplifications of Turkoman patterns.**

JOHN J. COLLINS JR. GALLERY.

LEFT **Veramin mafrash panel, 3ft. 5in. × 1ft. 3in., c. 1900. The large "X" motifs in the field were commonly used on the cross-panels of Turkoman ensis. The fringe clearly shows the variety of wools used in the warp of many tribal weavings.**

JOHN J. COLLINS JR. GALLERY.

BAKHTIARI AND LURI RUGS The Bakhtiari and Luri tribes live in the mountains and plains east of Isfahan to the Iraqi border. The Bakhtiari is one of the major tribes and the Luri is closely related to it.

All Luri rugs are of the nomadic type. Bakhtiari rugs are of both nomadic and village types. The nomadic pieces are mostly large bags, donkeybags, and kilims. The Bakhtiaris also owned villages in the area of their summer camp grounds in the Chahar Mahal. These two groups are considered as separate types. The technical characteristics of nomadic Bakhtiari and Luri rugs are:

Knot type: Symmetric.

GEORGE FINE KILIMS.

LEFT **Luri kilim, 4ft. 5in. × 7ft. 7in., c. 1800.** This abstractly patterned kilim shows many features of nomadic rugs: abrash, limited color range, irregular edges, and various colored warps.

ABOVE **Luri gabbeh rug, 3ft. 9in. × 5ft. 6in., c. 1900.** This gabbeh is less abstract than most in having a clearly defined medallion design, but the coarse knotting, multiple wefts, and design originality make it a gabbeh.

BELOW **Bakhtiari bagface, 2ft. 4in. × 2ft. 5in., c. 1890. A** superb example of Bakhtiari flatweaving, this is the face and one fourth of the back of a bag. Cotton is used for the white areas in these weavings.

JOHN J. COLLINS JR. GALLERY.

42

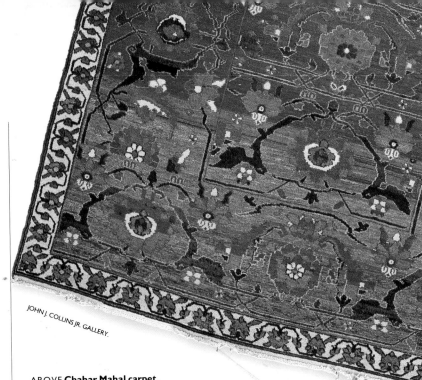

JOHN J. COLLINS JR. GALLERY.

Warp and weft fibers: Wool, with occasional use of goathair or cotton. Warps in Luri rugs are mostly natural browns, some mixed with white; in Bakhtiaris they are white with some natural brown mixed. Wefts in both are natural browns or red.

Edge finish: Mostly overcast in dark brown wool or goathair.

End finish: May be 1–3in., kilim weave, natural color or with stripes.

Dyes and colors: Dark blues predominate. Reds are light in tone and yellows are strong.

Technical features: In many large bags white cotton is used. Bag bottoms are woven in pile.

The Chahar Mahals are large carpets and rugs. The most common pattern is an all-over one of squares or lozenges with various trees and flowers in them. Their technical characteristics are:

Knot type: Symmetric.

Warp and weft fibers: Cotton, some blue-wefted.

Edge finish: Overcast in black wool.

End finish: Kilim weave of 1–2in.

Technical features: Inscriptions are frequently found in these rugs.

ABOVE **Chahar Mahal carpet, 5ft. 6in. × 6ft., c. 1890.** Although many Chahar Mahal carpets have similar patterning, unique pieces such as this one are highly collectible. The field and borders are covered with the herati border design. A few straight lines of the vine connecting the patterns are drawn to create a field demarcation. The abrashed blue and simple ivory border are especially effective.

JOHN J. COLLINS JR. GALLERY.

ABOVE **Bakhtiari rug, 4ft. × 8ft. 6in., c. 1880.** Garden designs are a recurring theme in Persian rugs and the combination of willows, cypresses and other flowering trees and shrubs are typical. The border pattern is often found in Caucasian rugs too.

JOHN J. COLLINS JR. GALLERY.

RIGHT **Chahar Mahal carpet, 3ft. 10in. × 5ft. 9in., c. 1900.** Two birds confronting a tree is an ancient symbol in weaving. The two-directional design of this small rug is highly unusual and original. The use of willow trees in the field corners is a clever resolution of a design problem.

RIGHT **Qashqai gabbeh rug,**
5ft. 1in. × 5ft. 10in., c. 1850.
Gabbeh rug designs call to
mind concepts of abstract
painting. Their appeal lies in
the saturated colors and the
observer's subjective response
to the design. It is only in
recent years that they have
come to the attention of
collectors.

BELOW **Qashqai donkeybag,**
4ft. 2in. × 2ft. 3in., c. 1890. This
piece exhibits the same design
and colors as the kilim on page
5 and shows how donkeybags
look when closed. The top
woven areas have slits through
which closure loops are passed.
Four are visible at the center.

JOHN J. COLLINS JR. GALLERY.

BELOW LEFT **Khamseh saddle**
cover, 1ft. 11in. × 3ft. 9in.,
c. 1880. Khamseh saddle covers
are rare. The slits for the
pommel and cantle of the
saddle clearly identify it as
such. Viewed from the other
side, without these, it could be
mistaken for a prayer rug.

PRIVATE COLLECTION.

JOHN J. COLLINS JR. GALLERY.

JOHN J. COLLINS JR. GALLERY

JOHN J. COLLINS JR. GALLERY

ABOVE **Qashqai bagface, 1ft. 10in. × 2ft., c. 1890. The medallion of this piece is the prototypical one found on many Qashqai weavings. The main border pattern is also common to the group.**

ABOVE **Khamseh bagface, 1ft. 10in. × 2ft. 1in., c. 1880. Khamseh chickens cover the field of this donkey bagface along with small octagons, botehs, and "S" motifs. The palette, dominated by several blues, is common to Khamseh weavings.**

JOHN J. COLLINS JR. GALLERY.

LEFT **Qashqai donkeybag, 1ft. 8in. × 8ft., c. 1880. This donkeybag is open as it would have been woven on the loom. It shows the dramatic patterns which may be found on some examples. To complete the donkeybag, the weaver would fold the pile faces over the center areas and sew the sides shut.**

ABOVE **Khamseh bagface, 1ft. 8in. × 1ft.11in., c. 1900. This medallion pattern is also found on rugs. As woven here, the bagface can be viewed as a miniature rug. Because of the limited space, the filler animals are not as carefully drawn as they would be in a larger weaving.**

QASHQAI AND KHAMSEH RUGS The Qashqai and Khamseh tribes live in southeastern Iran around the city of Shiraz. Their rugs have similar features. The Qashqai and Khamseh weavings are primarily small and area size rugs and they also produce many bags and utilitarian trappings. The patterns are mainly geometric and include a variety of animal, floral, and human forms as filler elements. The technical characteristics of Qashqai and Khamseh rugs are:

Knot type: Asymmetric, mostly open left, and symmetric.

Warp and weft fibers: Wool. Qashqai warps are mostly white, Khamseh mostly mixed brown and white. Qashqai wefts are natural or dyed red; Khamseh dyed red and brown.

Edge finish: Qashqai are overcast mostly in two colors of wool; Khamseh overcast or selvaged in dyed wool or natural brown.

End finish: Kilim weave, of 1–2in., frequently with twined or brocaded stripes.

Dyes and colors: All colors are used but notable are bright, clear reds, many shades of blue, gold as a minor color, and a good green.

Technical features: Many rugs have two or more narrow end borders with alternating dark blue and white squares.

Qashqai patterns and designs include a three-medallion type and repeated all-over patterns with diagonal coloration. They are generally more tightly woven than Khamseh rugs.

Khamseh patterns and designs include a distinctive "chicken" or vertical ribbons in white and dark blue. Most Khamseh rugs have a loose, pliable feel.

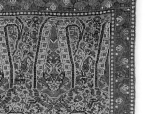

JOHN J. COLLINS JR. GALLERY.

ABOVE RIGHT **Khamseh rug, 4ft. 2in. × 6ft. 3in., c. 1880. This type of boteh with one or more smaller ones within it is called a "mother and child." It was often used by the Khamseh, but may also be seen in rugs from other regions.**

RIGHT **Khamseh rug, 3ft. 11in. × 7ft. 4in., c. 1880. These botehs are exceptionally large at about 1ft. 6in. high. This style of boteh comes from the shawl tradition of weaving. Note how they alternate facing right and left by rows.**

AFSHAR RUGS Afshars are from near the southern city of Kirman. Most of their rugs are small, but some are carpets. Some bags and utilitarian pieces were also woven. Afshar rugs divide into two groups, depending on whether wool is used for warps and wefts. They feature both geometric and floral patterns in medallion and all-over designs. The technical characteristics of Afshar rugs are:

Knot types: Asymmetric and symmetric, mostly open right.

Warp and weft fibers: Wool: white, occasionally mixed brown for warps; wefts wool, mostly orange-red or pink. Some warp depression. Cotton used for warps and/or wefts in later pieces.

Edge finish: Overcast with dyed wool.

End finish: Kilim weave of 1–6in. in natural color or dyed with stripes.

Dyes and colors: Reds are rust with strong yellow undertone; a salmon-orange secondary color is an identifying feature.

Technical features: Afshar wool has a dry touch and low luster.

BALUCHI RUGS Baluchi rugs come from the eastern region on the Afghanistan and Turkmenistan borders. Most rugs are small; many are in prayer rug format. They exhibit one of the darkest palettes in red and blue combined with dark brown and white outlining. Natural camelhair is common. The patterns are both floral and geometric. Large numbers of bags were also produced. The technical characteristics of Baluchi rugs are:

Knot type: Asymmetric open left, a few open right and some symmetric.

Warp and weft fibers: Warps are white wool; wefts are dark brown wool. Newer Baluchi rugs from Iran have cotton warps and wefts.

Edge finish: Selvage in brown wool or goathair.

End finish: Plain to elaborate 1–10-in, kilim in colored stripes or patterned with brocade techniques.

Technical features: Soft, lustrous wool and brilliant blues.

PRIVATE COLLECTION.

JOHN J. COLLINS JR. GALLERY.

ABOVE, TOP **Afshar bagface, 1ft. 7in. × 2ft. 5in., c. 1880.** The botehs of this bagface are elegantly drawn with their deeply curving tops. The predominance of blue and white is unusual, and the weave is exceptionally fine, giving great clarity to the patterns. For an Afshar the wool is softer and more lustrous than usual.

BELOW **Afshar mafrash panel, 3ft. 11in. × 1ft. 1in., c. 1890.** Many tribes weave mafrashs with pile patterned sides and ends. This is the side panel of such a bag. The main border is especially bold for Afshar weavings.

ABOVE **Afshar rug, 5ft. 3in. × 8ft. 3in., c. 1880.** The patterns and designs of this piece are typical of Afshar rugs. The three diamond medallions share a common heritage with Qashqai and Khamseh rugs as well.

JOHN J. COLLINS JR. GALLERY.

NORTHAMPTON LIBRARY

JOHN J. COLLINS JR. GALLERY.

SHAHSAVAN RUGS Shahsavans are woven in an area stretching from Tehran northward to the Azerbaijan border. Most are flatweaves. The patterns are geometric and in a wide variety of colors. Most weavings are storage bags, floor kilims, and covers. The patterns and designs are among the most interesting of those used for flatweaves.

ABOVE **Afshar rug, 3ft. 10in. × 6ft. 10in., c. 1900.** The colors, flatweave ends, and design of a floral lattice are typical of Afshar rugs.

BELOW **Shahsavan bagface, 1ft. 7in. × 1ft. 1in., c. 1850.** "Symbolic content" is one of the mysteries and fascinations for the collector. This medallion is filled with images of life, death, regeneration, and eternity. A beautiful and powerful design.

PETER PAP ORIENTAL RUGS, INC.   PHOTO GARY McKINNIS.

PRIVATE COLLECTION.

ABOVE **Shahsavan horse cover, 4ft. 1in. × 5ft. 7in., c. 1900.** Horse or animal covers have this unusual shape because the "arms" went around the chest of the animal to be secured.

This one is unusual in having been woven as one piece; most were produced in two pieces and sewn together.

VILLAGE RUGS

Some villages use designs and patterns in their rugs which have remained unchanged by commercial influences; these are the ones which are collected.

NORTHWESTERN VILLAGES Northwestern villages center on the city of Tabriz. The rugs in this region are woven with the Turkish knot.

Heriz has given its name to a group of rugs with a distinctive character in mostly room sizes. They are also known as Serapi, Bakshaish, Ahar, and Karaja. Most are decorative carpets and are bought as such. Few small rugs were made, and these appeal to collectors. They have medallions and all-over patterns and are woven with cotton warps and wefts.

Sarab produces a distinctive group of mostly runners. These have wide outer borders in natural camelhair or wool dyed the color of camelhair. The field has series of large, connected medallions. Pinks and blues are used in the patterns, which are geometric and floral. They have mostly wool warps and wefts.

ABOVE **Bakshaish carpet, 9 × 16ft., c. 1880.** Heriz district rugs with unusual medallions (as in this carpet), diffuse patterning and a salmon and blue coloration are usually called Bakshaish after a village in the district.

BELOW **Karaja rug, 5ft. 2in. × 6ft. 10in., c. 1900.** The two medallion types on this rug are found on most Karaja rugs, including runners. The weaver filled the field with an infinite variety of small patterns.

RIGHT **Serab rug, 2ft. 11in. × 8ft. 4in., c. 1910.** Rugs from several weaving areas with this coloration – light fields and plain, camel-colored outer borders – and several large, connected medallions are called Serab, after a village of that name.

LEFT **Heriz carpet, 7ft. 10in. × 10ft., c. 1910.** The colors of this carpet are typical of Heriz rugs from the first quarter of the twentieth century. The small medallion with large anchor pendants is unusual and sets this rug apart.

WEST IRAN West Iran is the most prolific rug-weaving region. The commercial rugs of Hamadan, Sarouk, Lilihan, and Seraband are from here. The Senneh, Bijar, and Chahar Mahal rugs mentioned above are made here.

Other village rugs of note originate from Maslaghan, Malayer, Sarouk, and Ferahan.

Maslaghan produced a medallion-design rug which is unlike any other Hamadan rug. Most are about 4 × 6ft. and single-wefted. They are woven with the symmetric knot and have cotton warps with either cotton or wool wefts. The large, angularly lobed medallion and field are patterned with small designs. The ground color of this medallion contrasts sharply with the color of the field. The borders are narrow. The result is a dramatic and bold design.

Malayer, Sarouk, and *Ferahan* are not far from one another. The patterns and quality of weave are among the best from this area. All have cotton warps and wefts, but differ in some technical characteristics.

Malayers are distinguished from Ferahans and Sarouks by having a single weft and symmetric knot. Most are 4 × 6ft. and have all-over and medallion designs. The boteh appears frequently. As a group they have never been well defined. One way of describing them is a Senneh rug without its characteristic feel.

Sarouks come in carpet and rug sizes. Medallion designs are the hallmark of this group. They are elegantly drawn with rounded outlines and filled with arabesques. Red, blue, and white are the predominating colors with occasional greens. They are finely and tightly woven.

Ferahans are not as finely woven as Sarouks. Ferahans have all-over patterns, particularly the herati. Medallions are used but they are more angular and without the rounded edges of those of Sarouks. They are noted for a particular shade of green which is corrosive. The pattern range of Ferahans is extensive.

PETER PAP ORIENTAL RUGS, INC. PHOTO GARY McINNIS.

JOHN J. COLLINS JR. GALLERY.

ABOVE **Sarouk mat, 1ft. 10in. × 2ft. 9in., c. 1930. This small mat is representative of the type of rug that was chemically treated and repainted a deeper** blue-red for the U.S. market. **An examination of the back of these rugs reveals a visibly light pink color.**

ABOVE **Sarouk carpet, 9ft. 1in. × 12ft. 4in., c. 1890. This type of lobed medallion with pendants was used on both small and** large rugs in Sarouk. Although **patterned with a curving, undulating floral meander, the corners are unreconciled.**

PETER PAP ORIENTAL RUGS, INC.

PETER PAP ORIENTAL RUGS, INC.

ABOVE **Sarouk carpet, 7ft. 2in. × 9ft., c. 1910. This unusual Sarouk, with architectural "pillars" supporting the arches on both ends of the field, shows several features of cartoon-derived design. These are curved lines, complex drawing of patterns, and reconciled corners. The abrash in the blue field creates a three-dimensional illusion.**

BELOW **Ferahan rug, 4ft. 6in. × 6ft. 10in., c. 1890. This rug is typical of Ferahans of the nineteenth century. The small areas of corrosive green and lavender are color identifiers. The field design is a combination of herati and gul-i-henna patterns. The vase of flowers (Zili Sultan) pattern of the main border was a common one.**

ABOVE **West Persian village rug, 4ft. 2in. × 6ft. 3in., c. 1890. Although the medallion is a Salor Turkoman gul, this is not a Turkoman rug. The weave, colors, and other patterns are typically west Persian. It illustrates how village weavers occasionally tried something out of the ordinary and created true folk art. Although dated, it is not drawn precisely enough to be legible.**

BELOW **Malayer rug, 4ft. 10in. × 7ft., c. 1900. Malayer rugs are often less citified than their Sarouk and Ferahan cousins. The weaver added a bit of whimsy with the animals at each end and the randomly placed flowers.**

PETER PAP ORIENTAL RUGS, INC.

PETER PAP ORIENTAL RUGS, INC. PHOTO GARY McKINNIS.

SOUTH IRAN South Iran has two village productions, which date only from the middle of this century. These are Abadeh and Yalemeh. Both types were developed for commercial markets and made by settled nomads. Although once common in the marketplace, they are no longer.

Abadehs take their patterns and designs from the Qashqai. The difference is that they are woven with cotton warp and wefts, the latter frequently dyed blue. They were made in small and area rug sizes, normally not larger than 6 × 9ft.

Yalemehs are more closely allied with the Khamseh patterns. The small rugs have multiple medallions ringed with latchhooks; the same medallions are arranged in a grid of borders in larger rugs and carpets. They are woven with wool warps and wefts, although cotton was also used for wefts.

EAST IRAN East Iran has only one village of note, Dorokhsh. Although some carpets were made, most are 4 × 6ft. and the boteh is the most common pattern. Red-orange is a characteristic color. They have an asymmetric knot and usually a single border. Prized by Persians, they have never had the same fascination for Western collectors.

CITY RUGS

Except for the central region where several cities are renowned for their carpets, only one city dominates the field in the north, south, and east – Tabriz, Kerman, and Mashhad, respectively.

TABRIZ Tabriz has been a center of weaving for centuries and it was largely from here that the great carpet boom of the nineteenth century began. All types, sizes, and designs are woven here. Wool and silk are used in Tabriz. Most rugs are woven on cotton foundations (with the exception of silk rugs) and both symmetric and asymmetric knots are used. Tabriz rugs have a characteristic feel: if the hand is placed under the rug on the back, stiff, bristle-like hairs may be felt.

PETER PAP ORIENTAL RUGS, INC.   PHOTO GARY McKINNIS.

JOHN J. COLLINS JR. GALLERY.

ABOVE, TOP **Yalameh rug, 5ft. 4in. × 8ft. 6in., c. 1950. Most Yalameh rugs display this type of medallion. This design clearly shows a Qashqai origin. Most examples have the medallions arranged within squares on the field.**

ABOVE **Abadeh rug, 4ft. 11in. × 7ft. 3in., c. 1930. A piece from the beginning of the Abadeh rug period. The pattern, a vase filled with flowers, known as Zili Sultan, is a common design throughout Iran.**

The most collectible rugs from Tabriz are of silk. A certain class of these is called Heriz silk. Although the patterns and designs of Heriz silk rugs are varied, one constant feature is the presence of unreconciled borders. If the borders are reconciled, the rug is known as a Tabriz rug. Silk rug designs include prayer rugs, pictorials, and medallions. Other Tabriz rugs with wool pile in these same patterns are also collected.

JOHN J. COLLINS JR. GALLERY.

PETER PAP ORIENTAL RUGS, INC. PHOTO GARY McKINNIS.

ABOVE **Tabriz carpet, 8ft. 10in. × 11ft. 9in., c. 1900.** In color and design this carpet is representative of many Tabriz weavings. The open, abrashed field is particularly effective with the light colors and small, delicate patterning.

BELOW **Tabriz rug, 4ft. 3in. × 6ft., c. 1900.** The sophistication of city design is shown in this small rug. The field has a detailed rendering of the herati design and the three ground colors of the borders going from dark to light give the illusion of different levels.

ABOVE **Lavar Kerman prayer rug, 3ft. 10in. × 6ft., c. 1850.** This wonderful piece shows the colors and design finesse of Kerman rugs called Lavar. The trees, flowers, and birds are realistically drawn.

BELOW **Kerman saddle cover, 3ft. × 3ft. 10in., c. 1880.** The boteh is one of the patterns found frequently on Kerman rugs. City weavers did produce a few utilitarian pieces, including saddle covers.

PETER PAP ORIENTAL RUGS, INC. PHOTO GARY McKINNIS.

PETER PAP ORIENTAL RUGS, INC. PHOTO GARY McKINNIS.

KERMAN Kerman is located in the south. Its rugs have been among the finest woven in the country. The most desired Kerman rug is called Ravar or Lavar, the name of a town nearby. They were noted for their fine weave, their rich and vibrant cochineal red, ivory, and gold colors and elegant medallions. They were woven mainly in carpet and rug sizes; and most collectors favour the prayer rugs.

MASHHAD Mashhad is located in the northwest and, except for one type, its rugs are of average quality. Cochineal red is the dominant red. Emogli rugs are usually woven of silk and were the finest workshop rugs made in Mashhad. They are almost always red with a dense floral arabesque design; medallions are sometimes used. Some rugs of this region were made on cotton foundations.

CENTRAL IRAN Several of the most famous rug-production centers are located in central Iran. One has been weaving for centuries; the others are relative newcomers.

Kashan is the oldest and most famous of these cities. Many of the most famous rugs in museums around the world are attributed to it. In overall quality it has been the most consistent producer in this century. Many designs are used but medallions have always been a *forte* of the designers of Kashan. The small rugs and Tree of Life prayer rugs are the focus of collectors.

Isfahan, Nain and *Qum* are newcomers to the high-quality city rug group. Silk, in whole or in part, figures prominently in the rugs of these cities. Except for all-silk carpets, they are woven on cotton warps and wefts with asymmetric knots. Although carpet sizes are made in all three cities, it is the smaller rugs for which they are best known. In creating a carpet industry in these places, designers were inspired by the sixteenth-century designs of Shah Abbas.

Qum rugs generally have an all-over pattern. A garden design is typical. Green is frequently used as a major color in the palette.

Isfahan and Nain rugs both exhibit ornate medallion designs and light colors such as pale blues and beiges. More dark reds and blues are used in Isfahan rugs than

in Nains. Silk is used in combination with wool for the pile of both. Generally, in Isfahans the entire petal of a rosette pattern will be woven in silk: in Nains the rosette is outlined in silk.

IRANIAN FLATWEAVES

Flatweaves are made by all of the nomadic weavers of Iran and by many of the village weavers. Each has its own characteristic features, patterns and techniques.

Shahsavan flatweaves are discussed on page 48. Most of these are woven using the soumak technique. Today most exist as bagfaces. They have an exceptional design repertoire and make interesting collections.

Qashqai flatweaves are woven in sizes of about 6 × 10ft. in slitweave and dovetail tapestry. They were made as floor rugs and coverings. The simple abstract design of many Qashqai kilims appeals to those who like modern art. Bags of various types in several flatweave techniques, were also produced.

Kurdish, Baluchi, and *Luri/Bakhtiari* flatweaves are known but have not yet become popular. Kurdish flatweaves are still waiting to be thoroughly studied. The flatweaves of the Baluchi are even darker than the rugs and are difficult to appreciate, but are among the most complexly woven flatweaves. Luri/Bakhtiari flatweaves enjoyed a burst of interest in the 1970s.

Of village flatweaves the two most notable are *Sennehs* and *Bijars*. Senneh kilims are the finest ever woven by Asian weavers. They have always been prized and collected. The best ones are those from before World War I because of their fineness; after that time they were woven on coarser cotton warps. The boteh and herati figure prominently as patterns. The finest examples have multicolored silk warps. They are mostly about 4 × 6ft. in size.

Bijar kilims are heavy and sturdy. They have the same large medallions as the rugs, but more simplified and with open red fields. Bijar weavers produced some carrying bags using a soumak technique. They have a heavy construction and Persianate patterns such as the mina khani, herati, and boteh.

BELOW **Kashan rug, 4ft. 4in. × 6ft. 10in., c. 1900. The shape of the medallions and floral patterning in the field of** **Kashans make them among the most elegant of all Persian city rugs. This is a typical design used from the late nineteenth century until the 1930s.**

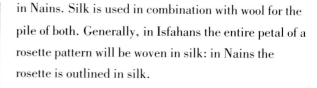
PETER PAP ORIENTAL RUGS, INC. PHOTO GARY McKINNIS.

PRIVATE COLLECTION.

THE RUGS OF CENTRAL ASIA

CHAPTER **6**

The rugs and weavings of Central Asia are tribal and nomadic, with the exception of Beshir rugs. The principal rug-weaving tribes were the Turkoman, Kazakhs, Uzbeks, Kirghiz, and Karakalpaks.

TURKOMAN RUGS

Turkoman rugs come in many different shades of red with all-over patterns of polygons called guls. Border patterns are geometric. Various types may be distinguished according to the shape of the gul, the shade of red used and the drawing of small patterns. Technical features further define the groups. The principal tribal divisions are Teke, Salor, Saryk, Yomud, Chodor, Ersari, and Beshir.

▌ *Types of weaving:* These are more varied than in any other weaving area. The most common ones are:

Main carpet: A rug for the floor.

Juval: A large storage bag. Sizes are 2–3 × 4–6ft.

Torba: A long, shallow storage bag about 1 × 3–5ft.

Mafrash: A smaller bag to hold personal items, about 1 × 2ft.

Khorjin: A term for a donkeybag.

Ensi: A rug to hang outside over the yurt entrance (the yurt being the portable dwelling of most Central Asian tribes). The field is divided into four panels with a fringe on only one end. The size is approximately 4 × 6ft.

Kaplyk: Shaped like an upside-down "U" and used on the inside of the yurt entrance.

Tentbands: Bands of various widths and lengths were made to construct the yurt, hold the covering felts in place and to serve as decoration.

ABOVE LEFT **Karakalpak ensi, 5ft. 2in. × 6ft. 2in., c. 1890. The Karakalpak attribution is based on a late nineteenth-century attribution for a rug of this type. Many attributions for Central Asian weavings remain** speculative. The designation ensi for this piece is based on its having a patterned kilim at one end and turned-under edge at the top. It does not exhibit the typical four-part field division of Turkoman ensis.

Asmalyk: A pentagonal or heptagonal weaving made as wedding trappings for the bridal camel.

Bride's rug: A small rug about 3 × 3ft. made by the bride to sit on at the wedding ceremony.

Patterns: The gul is the principal pattern. It has many different shapes and sizes and the interior motifs are varied. Some of guls used by the tribes are:

Teke gul: The best known of the Turkoman guls, this is rounded and connected vertically and horizontally by blue lines.

Salor gul: Also known as the turret gul because of the triangular projections around the edge, this is found on the carpets of the Teke, Saryk, and Ersari.

Gul-i-gul: There are many forms of this gul, which is used on Salor, Ersari, and Saryk rugs.

Juval or Saryk gul: Similar to the Teke gul but not connected by lines. It is used by most tribes.

Dyrnak gul: A diamond-shaped gul with hook projections around the edge.

Kepse gul: This diamond-shaped gul has bicolored, serrated panels on the edges. It is used only by the Yomud.

Tauk nuska gul: This, with two small animals in each gul quarter, is one of the most widely used and appears on the main carpets of most tribes.

Ertmen gul: Found primarily on Chodor carpets.

Secondary guls are important designs but are less directly related to specific tribes. Some of the common names for them are chemche, kurbage, Memling, erre, and sagdak.

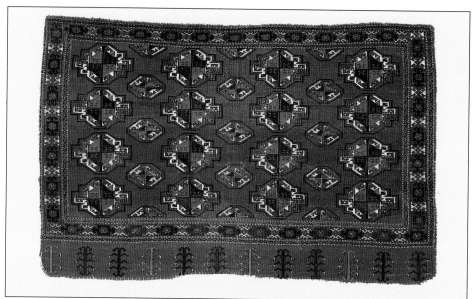

RIGHT **Salor juval, 2ft. 6in. × 4ft., c. 1840. The juval gul with small diamond secondary guls is most typical of Salor juvals. The bottom skirt or elem exhibits a stylized plant form. Small motifs within the guls are in pink and blue silk.**

PETER PAP ORIENTAL RUGS, INC.

RIGHT **Central Asian asmalyk, 4ft. 6in. × 1ft. 10in., c. 1890. Asmalyks, whose purpose was to decorate the bridal camel, were either pentagonal or hexagonal, and were made in pairs. Most asmalyks are attributed to the Yomuds. This one with a unique pattern is from an unknown tribal group.**

PRIVATE COLLECTION.

Non-gul and floral patterns are found on the field and borders of rugs called Beshir. These are not considered to be nomadic. Many of the patterns are Persianate or derived from textiles such as ikats.

■ *Colors* are important in distinguishing between the weavings of different tribes. The reds used cover a wide spectrum – for example, there are brown-red, rust-red, mid-reds, purple-red, and purple. The blues used are mostly very dark blue or blue-black; mid- and light blues are rare. Yellow occurs in many shades from light to strong in intensity. Blue-green is found frequently as a secondary color. Natural white and brown wool is used.

■ *Technical features* used in determining a tribal attribution are: type of major and secondary gul (on main carpets); type of knot; knot density; warp and weft wool color; warp depression; color of red; edge finish; special features.

TEKE RUGS have the Teke gul; an asymmetric knot open to the right; a knot density of more than 150 per square inch; mainly white wool warps; warps on one level; a bright mid-range red; overcast edges: and a short, velvety texture.

SALOR RUGS exhibit the Salor, juval, and gul-i-guls; an asymmetric knot open to the left; a knot density of more than 150 per square inch; white wool warps; deep warp depression; mostly bright, rich reds; red and blue selvage; and minor use of pink-red silk.

PRIVATE COLLECTION.

JOHN J. COLLINS JR. GALLERY.

ABOVE **Yomud ensi, 4ft. 1in. × 5ft. 5in., c. 1870. Ensis are directional in design and have one or two elems at the bottom, as in this one. The field is divided into two panels, often with rows of Y-shaped** patterns. **Yomud rugs frequently include a dark purple-red with a contrasting bright red, as in this piece.**

PRIVATE COLLECTION.

ABOVE **Teke main carpet, 6ft. 5in. × 10ft. 5in., c. 1850. This carpet displays the Teke gul and its characteristic connecting vertical and horizontal lines. The elements may be either plain tapestry weave or pile as here.**

RIGHT **Saryk main carpet, 7ft. 10in. × 8ft. 9in., c. 1870. Because it was frequently used on Saryk main carpets, the juval gul is also called the Saryk gul. In Saryk weavings the "X" pattern is often used for the main border of this carpet.**

SARYK RUGS have the juval, Salor, and gul-i-guls; a symmetric knot; a knot density of more than 100 per square inch; mainly white wool warps; depressed warps; rust-, mahogany-, and purple-reds; red and blue selvage in early rugs, overcast edges in later rugs; a short pile with white cotton and pink-red silk.

YOMUD RUGS have the dyrnak, kepse, and tauk nuska guls; both symmetric and asymmetric knots; a knot density of more than 100 per square inch; white to gray wool warps; warps mostly on one level; all types of reds; selvage and overcast edges; white-ground main border; curled leaf pattern for main border; and cotton or part-cotton wefts.

CHODOR RUGS have the ertmen and tauk nuska guls; asymmetric and symmetric knots; a knot density of more than 80 per square inch; brown or brown/white mixed wool and other animal hair fibers; some warp depression; purple, brown and mid-reds; red and blue selvage; medium length pile; dry-feeling wool; cotton or part-cotton wefts and mostly white-ground main borders.

ERSARI RUGS have the gul-i-gul and tauk nuska guls; an asymmetric knot mostly open to the right; a knot density of more than 70 per square inch; white to gray warps; warps on one level or slightly depressed; bright to rust-reds; brown selvage; use of yellow as a minor color; loose, heavy handle; and lustrous wool.

BESHIR RUGS have non-gul patterns; asymmetric knots mostly open to the right; a knot density more than 50 per square inch; white, gray, and brown warps on one level; medium and rust-reds; brown, blue and red selvage; much yellow; and loose, heavy handle.

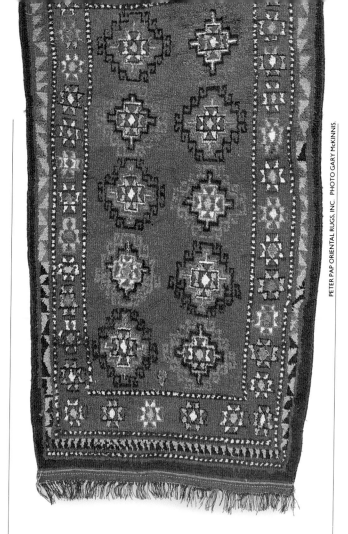

PETER PAP ORIENTAL RUGS, INC. PHOTO GARY McKINNIS.

ABOVE **Uzbek rug, 2ft. 10in. × 4ft. 3in., c. 1900.** The border patterns and colors are typical of an undefined but specific group of Uzbek weavers.

DENNIS AND MAILE MARQUAND. PHOTO GARY McKINNIS.

RIGHT **Uzbek rug, 3ft. 4in × 3ft 6in., c. 1880.** This julhir, or sleeping rug, is made of four separate strips sewn together. It was probably woven by a different Uzbek tribe from the rug shown in the illustration above. It bears a strong resemblance to the gabbeh rugs of Iran.

TURKOMAN FLATWEAVES

Their flatweaves are the least known of the Turkoman weavings. They served specific functions and have a design repertoire of their own. Some of the more notable types of flatweave are:

Main carpets: The Yomud, Teke, and Ersari produced large flatwoven rugs. The most common technique used is cicim with a simple four-part kotshak design within a lattice. The weave varies from coarse in Ersari pieces to very fine in Yomud and Teke ones. Another design is horizontal bands with mihrab or arch shapes in them. These are attributed to the Yomud and Teke.

Juvals, torbas, and donkeybags: On juvals the Memling gul is used; on smaller bags, all-over small pattern repeats are found.

Tentbands: Some bands have patterns woven in pile on a flatweave ground. Others are weft- or warp-faced patterns. These were woven in various widths and lengths.

Kilims: Both the dovetail and slit tapestry techniques were used. The few known examples have been attributed to the Yomud and Ersari.

OTHER CENTRAL ASIAN WEAVINGS

The Uzbeks, Karakalpaks, Kirghiz, and Kazakhs did not weave enough rugs for them to be commercially important in the West. Their weavings are more coarsely knotted. Most are nomadic in style and were woven without commercial consideration. The Memling gul is a pattern frequently seen.

Some of these tribes wove a type of rug, unique to them, called a julhir. This served as a sleeping rug. Julhirs are woven as one piece or constructed of several strips sewn together.

Most of the tribes, however, used their wool for the production of felts instead of woven articles. Felt was made into many types of article. Many Kazakh, Kirghiz, and Karakalpak woven articles have patterns directly related to felt patterns.

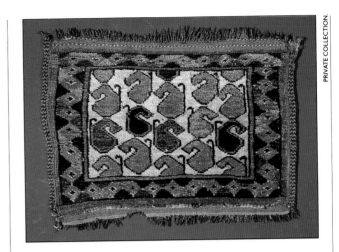

PRIVATE COLLECTION.

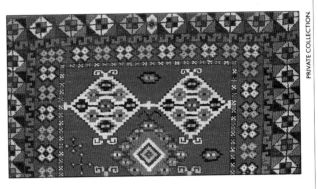

PRIVATE COLLECTION

ABOVE, TOP **Uzbek torba, 1ft. 3in. × 1ft. 8in., c. 1880.** Uzbek weavings are made in the same shapes as Turkoman, but their colors and patterns are different and less dominated by gul patterns. This small piece exhibits an unusual boteh pattern with brilliant, simple colors.

ABOVE **Uzbek rug, 86 × 130cm (2ft 10in × 4ft 3in), c. 1900.** The pattern on this small rug possibly derives from a type of Central Asian silk fabric called ikat. The border patterns and colours are typical of an undefined but specific group of Uzbek weavers.

UZBEK WEAVING may be the most extensive after the Turkoman. There were Uzbek groups that were tribal and nomadic, such as the Lakai, but many groups were settled and mixed with the Turkoman. A definition of Uzbek weaving would include the following characteristics:

Patterns: The patterns used are derived from Turkoman weavings, but they are simplified and not as precisely drawn as the originals.

Warp and weft fibers: Most have dark brown wool warps and wefts and these threads are not spun as finely nor as tightly as in Turkoman weaving. Cotton may be used for wefts.

NORTHAMPTON COLLEGE LIBRARY

ABOVE **Kirghiz rug, 3ft. 5in. ×
7ft. 8in., c. 1920. A palette
limited to four colors – red,
blue, brown, and yellow – is
common to a group of Kirghiz
rugs. This piece displays a**
**highly simplified version of the
mina khani pattern. The main
border pattern shows the
influence of East Turkestan and
China.**

Knot type: Both symmetric and asymmetric knots are
used.

Knot density and depression: The knot density is
among the coarsest. Warp depression is not used.

Dyes and colors: The reds tend to brown. Yellow is
used in larger field or pattern areas. A gold or gold-
orange occurs frequently.

Edge finish: Brown wool selvage.

End finish: Kilim ends are more loosely woven than
Turkoman ones.

Most Uzbek weavings are floor rugs, but they also
wove utilitarian pieces including juvals and torbas.
Their tentbands are mostly about 4in. wide and of
varying lengths with weft-faced patterning.

KARAKALPAK WEAVING is well documented. Most of
this tribe's weavings seem to be small bags or strips,
which were made into bags. A large number of
tentbands in several mixed techniques are definitely
attributed to the Karakalpaks.

The major pile article is the napramach, a
rectangular weaving about 1 × 3ft. This has closely
spaced guls with interior patterns similar to Turkoman
ones. Older pieces have a bright, clear red, while dark,
purplish browns constitute the second most important
color.

Most of the pieces are edged with a rather heavy
selvage, which may be natural wool or dyed. They serve
a variety of functions; many were sewn together with
flatwoven bands to create bags and covers.

KIRGHIZ WEAVING is the best-documented weaving
of these lesser-known tribes. The Kirghiz wove rugs
and a variety of different bags in knotted pile. If guls
were used on these Kirghiz rugs, they were generally
large, and a 5 × 9-ft. rug may have only three or four
in the field instead of several rows as in Turkoman rugs.
Many of the patterns are small all-over ones of
geometrically drawn flowers. Most rugs are twice as
long as they are wide, with selvages. The fringe is
braided and about 6–10in. long. Both symmetric and
asymmetric knots are used. The knot density is 20–50
per square inch. There may be one or two wefts
between each row of knots. Rust-red is important, with
significant use of dark brown; yellow and white are
minor colors. Certain types of rug may be simply red
and blue, with brown used only for outlines.

The bags are mostly squarish in shape, about 2 ×
2ft., and exhibit many of the same patterns that are
used on the rugs. Most have a single border or a second
minor one used on the outside. The Kirghiz also wove
napramach and tentbands in a variety of techniques
and sizes.

KAZAKH WEAVING is from the northernmost of these
peoples, who in fact produced the fewest woven
articles. The largest they made were flatweaves,
compound weavings with large areas of plain tapestry
crossed by wide bands with areas of brocading, extra-
weft patterning, and twining. Several wide bands have
three or four simple geometric forms within them
alternating with smaller bands of repeating patterns.
Red is the predominant color, with black and white as
the major accents.

Tentbands and donkeybags were woven using several
different techniques. These were cut into pieces of
equal length, sewn together and used as floor coverings
and bedroll covers.

PETER PAP ORIENTAL RUGS, INC.   PHOTO GARY McINNIS.

THE RUGS OF CHINA, EAST TURKESTAN, AND TIBET

CHAPTER **7**

The rugs of China, East Turkestan, and Tibet are normally considered together because the influence of the Chinese design tradition is evident in all of them. However, each area is different, with its own traditions of design, color, and weave.

CHINESE RUGS

Chinese rugs display patterns and colors found in other Chinese arts such as textiles, wood carving, and ceramics. The craft of rug weaving was probably brought into China with the invasions from Mongolia. It is only in the colder climates north of the Yellow River that sheep are raised and rugs are woven.

The Chinese used rugs primarily as floor and furniture coverings. A special kind of rug was woven to fit around columns in palaces and monasteries. Another type of weaving is the saddle cover. Chinese rugs were woven in workshops and are treated as city rugs. Their principal characteristics are:

▌ *Patterns:* Primarily floral. These are used in combination with the dragon, phoenix, and other auspicious symbols represented by animals, fruits, and flowers. A group of geometric patterns are used in both border and field, such as a fret, the pearl, writing symbols, and a rice pattern.

▌ *Designs:* Both all-over and centred. One of the most typical is a floral medallion with small sprigs of flowers in the field. The centre of the medallion may have dragons, phoenixes, or Fo dogs (Buddha's guards).

▌ *Colors:* Vary according to the period when they were woven, but the most common are blue, ivory, and yellow. Red is rarely seen in Chinese rugs; the only colors from the red range are pinks and salmons. Shades of brown were used in small-pattern areas.

The dominant color in the oldest Chinese rugs – for

ABOVE, LEFT **Chinese chair back, 2ft. 4in. × 2ft. 1in., c. 1880. Rugs with this scalloped edge at the top and borders, and a field design drawn to fit the space, were made to cover the back of a chair. They had companion pieces which covered the seat. The dragon is a common theme.**

PETER PAP ORIENTAL RUGS, INC.

ABOVE **Peking rug, 4ft. 5in. ×
6ft. 6in., c. 1880.** The colors
ivory and blue are typical of
Peking rugs from the turn of
the century. The motifs on the
field are clearly recognizable
items from everyday life. The
floral medallion and border
patterns are universal ones in
Chinese rugs.

BELOW **Chinese rug, 2ft. 4in. ×
4ft. 1in., c. 1880.** The blue and
yellow palette of this small
piece is typical of many
nineteenth-century Chinese
rugs. The pattern is a cloud
lattice and the same as that on
the Khotan rug shown in the
illustration on page 63.

BRIAN AND STEPHANIE MOREHOUSE COLLECTION.

example, of the early nineteenth century — was yellow.
A corrosive brown is found in the early rugs. Blue
became dominant during the course of the nineteenth
century. At the turn of the twentieth century the
clipping of pattern outlines began, and this is found in
almost all Chinese rugs from the 1920s onward.

AREAS OF PRODUCTION Ning Hsia produced rugs
with yellow as a major color. Paotou rugs were
predominantly blue with ivory. Peking rugs were room-
size with blue fields and ivory or gold borders. Early in
the twentieth century Tiensien, the port for Peking,
became a major commercial carpet center. The
technical features of all of these rugs are:

Knot type: Asymmetric.

Knot density: The oldest pieces are the coarsest at
about 40–70 knots per square inch. Mid- and late
nineteenth-century rugs have 60–90 knots in the same
area.

Warp and weft fibers: Cotton was used for both and
undyed.

Edge finish: In early pieces a selvage was used.
Later a cotton overcast was used.

End finish: Only about 1in. of kilim was woven. The
fringe was not more than 5in.

Rug sizes: Most are carpets. Smaller rugs, chair-seat
and chair-back covers were produced in Paotou and
Ning Hsia.

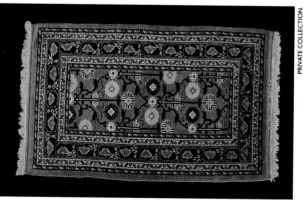

PRIVATE COLLECTION.

ABOVE **Khotan rug, 2ft. 6in. ×
4ft. 4in., c. 1900.** A flower
within a lattice is a pattern
common to many rug-weaving
areas, but colors define East

Turkestan rugs as much as
design. The light rust-red, mid-
blue, and yellow would be hard
to find in other areas.

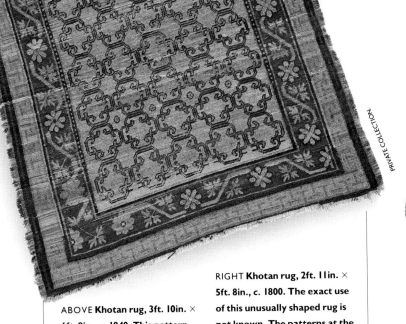

PRIVATE COLLECTION.

ABOVE **Khotan rug, 3ft. 10in. × 6ft. 8in., c. 1840.** This pattern comes from China and is called a cloud lattice. It creates two forms in the field: a cross and an eight-pointed star. The inner border of a rosette and leaves is unique to East Turkestan.

RIGHT **Khotan rug, 2ft. 11in. × 5ft. 8in., c. 1800.** The exact use of this unusually shaped rug is not known. The patterns at the ends are waves and mountains. Eight cloud patterns surround a fret medallion in the field. The red color of this rug is unusual for both Chinese and East Turkestan rugs.

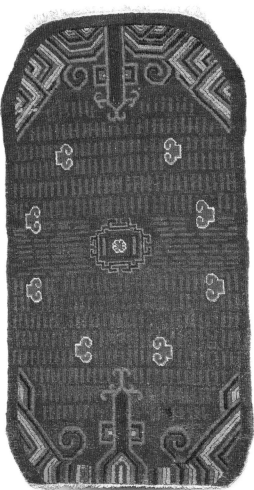

BRIAN AND STEPHANIE MOREHOUSE COLLECTION.

EAST TURKESTAN RUGS

East Turkestan rugs are from Xinjiang, the westernmost province of China, also called East Turkestan. The native population is Turkic, not Han Chinese. Rugs have been woven here for centuries, mostly in workshops. East Turkestan rugs differ from all others in patterns and colors. They reflect the influence of Islamic, Buddhist, and Chinese cultures. Their principal characteristics are:

▌ *Patterns:* Floral and abstract. A unique rosette in these rugs is called the coffered gul. A pattern not found elsewhere is the vase/pomegranate pattern. Chinese frets and wave patterns are used. Rugs from the end of the nineteenth century have Turkoman guls.

▌ *Designs:* Both all-over and centred. A common centered design is three round medallions. The medallions may have Chinese floral patterns or coffered guls. This type of design is Buddhist in origin. The vase/pomegranate is used as an all-over design. Coffered guls are used as all-over patterns. Some pieces have Persianate medallion and all-over patterns.

▌ *Colors:* Mainly pastel tones. Yellow was used frequently. A strong green is sometimes found. The browns are usually natural and not corrosive.

AREAS OF PRODUCTION Rug weaving is assigned to Khotan, Yarkand, and Kashgar based on design and structural features. The most prolific production is attributed to Khotan and includes all patterns. Silk rugs are usually attributed to Yarkand and Kashgar. The principal features of the rugs of East Turkestan are:

Knot type: Asymmetric

Knot density: May be 40–90 knots per 6.5 square inch. Silk rugs have a higher density.

Warp and weft fibers: Warps are cotton. Wefts may be cotton and wool. Most have three passes of the weft between each row of knots.

Edge finish: Overcast, but selvages occur.

End finish: Normally a kilim of 1–2in.

Rug sizes: Wide runners whose length is two to two and a half times their width, room-size carpets, and a few prayer rugs. Few utilitarian pieces were woven, most being saddle covers and donkeybags.

PRIVATE COLLECTION.

TIBETAN RUGS

Tibetan rugs have strong colors. Most of the patterns are Chinese-inspired or relate to Buddhism. They are essentially village weavings.

The weaving technique is unique. They are woven by a looping technique in which the pile threads are looped over a thin rod. When a row is finished, the loops are cut. The knots resulting from this looping may be asymmetric, symmetric or other versions of knots. Most Tibetan rugs are made for sitting, sleeping and praying, though some column and door rugs are woven. Many saddle blankets and some utilitarian pieces are also produced. The principal characteristics of Tibetan weavings are:

▌ *Patterns:* Floral, representational and abstract. Representational patterns are the dragon, phoenix, snow lion, tiger, and bat. Abstract and geometric patterns are squares, disks, and many of the same ones found in Chinese rugs.

▌ *Designs:* Both all-over and centred. The drawing is often cruder than in Chinese rugs. Many rugs have borders only on the ends.

▌ *Colors:* Generally very bright. This is due to the use of synthetic dyes. Red is the dominant color. Orange, blue, and yellow are also used as ground colors.

ABOVE **Khotan rug, 3ft. 3in. × 5ft. 8in., c. 1910. This rug illustrates several East Turkestan patterns. The circular medallion is derived from the Buddhist tradition and is frequently used. At its center and surrounding it are coffered guls, an East Turkestan pattern. The corners have the shou design from the Chinese culture.**

BELOW **Tibetan saddle cover, 3ft. 6in. × 2ft. 2in., c. 1910. Tibetan saddle covers are made in two shapes: this is a butterfly type. The animal is a snow lion, a common motif in Tibetan rugs.**

PRIVATE COLLECTION.

PETER PAP ORIENTAL RUGS, INC.

ABOVE **Tibetan saddle cover, 2ft. 3in. × 4ft., c. 1900.** This is the notched-corner style of saddle cover. The patterns are all derived from **Chinese** weaving. The red felt edging is the normal finish for Tibetan rugs.

BELOW **Tibetan mat, 2ft. × 2ft. 8in., c. 1910.** This small sitting mat displays many of the auspicious animals found in Tibetan rugs: dragons, tigers, snow lions, and phoenixes. The drawing of Tibetan rug patterns has a folklife quality.

BELOW, RIGHT **Tibetan pillar rug, 1ft. × 2ft. 4in., c. 1900.** This small rug with tiger stripes was hung at the entrance of a temple. The edges were sewn together to create a tube and then suspended. Like many Tibetan rugs it has borders only at the ends.

AREAS OF PRODUCTION The cities of Xigaze and Gyangze are the largest centers, but rug weaving is practised in most parts of the country. The principal technical features of the rugs are:

Knot type: Cut loop knot.

Knot density: May be 30–100 knots per square inch.

Warp and weft fibers: Warps are always wool. Wefts may be wool or cotton. Rugs with cotton are generally not as old as those with wool warps and wefts.

Edge finish: Many do not have typical edge finishes but are simply edge warps and wefts because felt edges and backing were added. If present, both simple selvedge and overcasting may be used.

End finish: About 1in. of kilim.

Rug sizes: There are many sizes. Tibetan rugs are classified by size in the following way:

TYPE	SIZE (approximate)
Sleeping rug (khaden)	3 × 6ft.
Sitting mat (khagangma)	3 × 3 ft.
Doorway rug (goyo)	4 × 5ft.
Large floor rug (saden)	6 × 9ft.
Pillar rug (kathum)	3 × 6ft.
Chair-seat and back rug (thigyarbya)	
Saddle rug (makden and masho) bottom and top pieces; and animal forehead decoration (tekheb)	6 × 6ft.

PRIVATE COLLECTION.

PRIVATE COLLECTION.

65

BLACK MOUNTAIN LOOMS, INC.

COLLECTIBLES, NONCOLLECTIBLES, AND THE NEW COLLECTIBLES

CHAPTER 8

In the mid-1960s a rebirth of interest in Oriental rugs began in the U.S. It started in large part because of a small group of men who had begun collecting during the Depression of the 1930s. Joseph McMullan, McCoy Jones, Arthur Jenkins, and others in the Hajji Baba Club, the first American rug society, had been collecting mostly nomadic and village rugs of the nineteenth century. This emphasis was a change from earlier periods; these men focused on rugs that they believed best represented the indigenous culture of their countries of origin, not the culture of the courts that inspired the classical carpets that earlier collectors had esteemed. Thus nomadic and tribal rugs, the use of natural dyes, and rugs not made for sale to Western markets became the dominant themes in Oriental rug collecting in the United States and Europe, although many Europeans retain a preference for classical rugs.

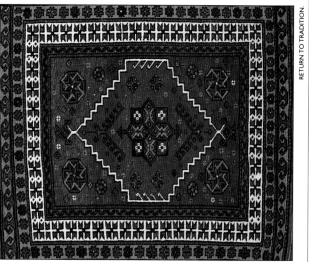

RETURN TO TRADITION.

ABOVE, LEFT **Kentwilly carpet, 9ft. 8in. × 10ft. 7in., woven 1993.** Kentwilly is a trademark name for handspun, natural-dye rugs woven in Turkey. The patterns are derived from Sultanabad district Persian rugs. Originality, abrash, and non-standard sizes typical of village weaving from the turn of the century distinguish these rugs from most new productions.

ABOVE **DOBAG rug, 3ft. 5in. × 4ft. 7in., woven 1993.** DOBAG rugs began the revival of natural-dye weaving in Turkey. They are trademarked with guaranteed quality standards and buyers receive certificates identifying the weaver of each rug. In this example the weaver's initials, "MM," are woven in the lower left corner of the field.

PETER PAP ORIENTAL RUGS, INC. PHOTO GARY McKINNIS.

PRIVATE COLLECTION.

LEFT Senneh rug, 5ft. × 6ft. 10in., c. 1890. This design of a floral medallion with a number of large floral sprays can be found on several types of rugs from Persia. The open field and white ground of field and border are unusual. The weave identifies this rug as Senneh.

ABOVE Senneh mat, 1ft. 9in. × 3ft. 1in., c. 1900. The colors (rust-red and blue-green) and pattern (herati) of this small mat are typical of Senneh weaving. Many such mats were woven. This one, which is wider warpways than weftways, is unusual.

With the new criteria whole classes of rugs became noncollectible. City rugs in particular were dismissed because they were commercial products. Any rug that had been chemically treated and painted was out. Rugs with obvious synthetic dyes that ran, or that collectors believed were synthetic, lost favor. No new rugs were being woven that could even qualify as future collectibles. Many collectors preferred to have no rug on the floor to one with synthetic dyes.

Rugs that collectors early in the century believed were highly desirable were no longer so regarded. The Ghiordes, Kula, and Bergama rugs so avidly collected, published and exhibited by Franklin Ballard fell in price. Ballard was the most "public" collector between the two world wars and the donation in 1922 of his collection to the Metropolitan Museum of Art remains the museum's foundation, but Ferahans, Sennehs, and Keshans, considered by many people to be the finest Persian rugs, were avoided by these new collectors as too commercial. The resale market for such rugs virtually dried up in 1940s, 1950s, and early 1960s.

Rugs that had been bought as good, cheap floor Orientals by grandparents gradually became the new focus. The Kazaks and Kubas of the Caucasus were recognized for their color and abstract art qualities. Turkoman rugs were perceived as the finest and most complex weaving of nomadic tribes. Baluchi rugs, which had been loss leaders in rug stores fifty years earlier, were admired for their wool and simplicity of design. Times change and collecting changes; prices go up and down.

It appeared for many years that the only rugs that collectors would consider were those made no later than the end of the nineteenth century. This attitude began to change in the 1980s with the revival of natural dyeing in Turkey. Many collectors are now buying rugs for their dyes and traditional and contemporary pattern innovation. Today natural-dyed rugs are being woven in several countries. These weavings and antique rugs are almost certain to be sought by the collectors of the future. Several countries are currently producing new natural-dye rugs.

NORTHAMPTON COLLEGE
LIBRARY

WOVEN LEGENDS, INC.

RIGHT **Azeri carpet, 9ft. 11in. × 14ft. 3in., woven 1993. Azeri is a trademark name for handspun, natural-dye rugs woven in Turkey. The patterns are derived from Heriz district Persian rugs. The weavers are encouraged to use individual artistic expression of their own in weaving within specified design concepts.**

Turkey is where the rebirth of natural dyeing started, and where it is strongest today. DOBAG, the acronym for a project to revive nineteenth-century village patterns and natural dyes, was the first and principal stimulus for the revival in western Turkey. Because of DOBAG's success other weavers in nearby villages began to produce similar rugs. They acquired the name Ayvacik, from a principal village of the region.

Today there are many classes of rugs and flatweaves being woven in western, central, and eastern Turkey with naturally dyed fibres. An economic boom has been created for the weavers and a stimulus to rug buying produced in the West. Because new rugs, even natural-dyed ones, have a flat, sometimes dull surface, many

are subjected to the same type of light chemical wash, that was common at the turn of the century, to soften their colors and put a sheen on the wool.

In eastern Turkey rugs with Iranian patterns from the Heriz area are woven in workshops. Handspun wool and natural dyes are used. The weavers are provided with cartoon patterns, but encouraged to improvize on these and so produce rugs with great vitality. These are marketed under the name Azeri.

Iran has been slow to join the natural-dye revival. However, in the past five years a new group of rugs has appeared on the market using natural dyes and handspun yarns. They are Gabbehs, traditional, colorful, minimally patterned Qashqai rugs, woven

WOVEN LEGENDS, INC.

ZOLLANVARI AG

ABOVE **Gabbeh rug, 6ft. 6in. ×
7ft. 6in., woven 1992. New
gabbeh rugs from south Persia
are being woven with natural
dyes and handspun wools. The**
weavers use designs from the
traditional abstract gabbehs
and pictorials, as in this
example. Most are squarish
instead of rectangular in shape.

ABOVE **Azeri folklife rug, 6ft.
10in. × 9ft. 5in., woven c. 1993.
The folklife rugs are pictorial
and each is completely original.
The weavers create scenes**
from everyday village life. This
rug depicts herds of sheep and
cows, a scene of a pageant play,
a family at a picnic, and many
other activities.

ZOLLANVARI AG

near Shiraz by Qashqai and other weavers. Gabbeh
rugs are coarsely woven and are used by the Qashqai
themselves. Twenty years ago few people had heard of
Gabbehs; today old and new ones have become
favored by collectors for their plain, simple patterns
and bright colours.

The new Gabbeh is woven in the traditional way.
There is a slight change in the sizes of the rugs, which
are squarer than the originals. Because of their
adherence to a traditional form, natural dyes, and
handspun wool, they fit in with the older weaving
tradition of the Persian nomadic style. It seems likely
that the use of natural dyes will be adapted elsewhere
in Iran as the success of the Gabbeh rugs spreads to
other regions of the country.

ABOVE **Gabbeh kilim, 6ft. 5in. ×
8ft. 2in., woven 1993. The same
weavers produce kilims in
nontraditional designs. This**
one echoes several pattern
themes found in kilims from
south Persia.

YAYLA TRIBAL RUGS.

ABOVE **Ersari Weaving Project rug, 5ft. 1in. × 6ft. 5in., woven 1993. Rugs of this type are** woven in Pakistan by refugees from Afghanistan using handspun wool and natural dyes. The patterns are taken from antique Beshir and Ersari Turkoman rugs.

Afghanistan weavers had begun to reuse natural dyes in the 1970s, but this trend was halted by the war with Russia. Among refugee weavers in Pakistan efforts were made to revive the use of natural dyes and patterns from nineteenth-century rugs, especially the Ersari and Beshir ones. This effort is still in its infancy and the production is small.

Tibet has seen a rebirth of natural-dye weaving as well. The production is centred in Lhasa in workshops, where traditional designs and patterns are used. Most of the sizes being woven are the sitting and sleeping rug types, though some room-size rugs are also made.

As the Turkish project has proved, the use of natural dyes and handspun wools has great appeal in Western markets. This benefits the weavers and satisfies the demands of collectors for rugs made by pre-synthetic and noncommercial methods. Because they are identical in almost all ways to nineteenth-century rugs, it seems likely that these are the new collectibles of the future just as the new Kazaks, Qashqais, Mujars, and Yomuds were the new collectibles of the late nineteenth century, though no one knew it.

To date many collectors continue to avoid rugs with synthetic dyes. However, as the price of increasingly fewer nineteenth-century rugs goes up, many people may find it acceptable to start collecting the rugs from the first half of the twentieth century. Although they have synthetic dyes, they still exhibit many of the same qualities of design, color, and use that collectors generally find desirable. Careful selection among these pieces for the best ones could result in fine collections at prices significantly below those of antique rugs. Individuals who like to stay ahead of the game may already be quietly pursuing this route.

INNER ASIA TRADING CO.

ABOVE **Tibetan Gangchen rug, 4 × 6ft., woven 1993. Most new "Tibetan" rugs are made in Nepal. These are made in Tibet with 100 percent Tibetan wool and the finest synthetic dyes.** The designs are taken directly from old Tibetan weavings. This is the chrysanthemum and vine pattern, which was widely used on old sleeping (khaden) rugs.

DENNIS AND MAILLE MARQUAND. PHOTO GARY McKINNIS.

ON BECOMING A COLLECTOR

CHAPTER **9**

Oriental rugs have been collected since the craft of rug weaving developed. In the Middle East where most are produced, they were initially collected by weavers and others as one way of holding wealth. In bad times they were sold as needed. In Europe and the United States, it was not until the late nineteenth century that collecting rugs became a pastime on a par with amassing painting, sculpture, and other art forms. The first wave of collecting focused entirely on classical carpets or pieces woven before 1800. The Fricks, Havemeyers, and Rockefellers bought them for their homes in New York, Newport, and elsewhere. Ordinary Americans purchased the new rugs from Turkey, the Caucasus, and Persia.

In Europe great collections were amassed. Baron Thyssen and Calouste Gulbenkian formed two great private collections. Museum curators in Berlin, London, Vienna, and Budapest bought and created the greatest museum collections of Oriental rugs from the fifteenth through the eighteenth centuries. Europeans had been buying Oriental rugs for centuries and continued to do so. Men of lesser means such as Ballard, Williams, and McMullan collected the rugs of the nineteenth century as well as classical ones.

This buying-and-collecting spree lasted until the Depression of the 1930s. When World War II ended and world economies began to recover, there were different responses in Europe and the U.S. In the United States people threw away or stored in attics their old Orientals and bought the new wall-to-wall carpeting. In Europe, where large numbers of rugs were destroyed during the war, they stuck with Oriental rugs. European dealers came to the U.S., bought the discarded rugs, and shipped them back to Europe.

ABOVE, LEFT **Uzbek soumak bag, 3 × 3ft., c. 1900. The same Uzbek weavers also made large donkeybags and floor rugs using the soumak technique. This is half of a donkeybag. The eight-pointed star is a common pattern in these soumaks. The arrangement and color use in the field are very similar to those of a group of Qashqai pile weavings.**

WOVEN LEGENDS, INC.

RIGHT **Turkish kilim, 4ft. × 6ft. 4in., new. This kilim, woven with handspun wool and dyed with natural dyes, is typical of many new types being produced in Turkey today. Their designs are usually taken from nineteenth-century weavings.**

Until the mid-twentieth century most people who collected rugs were generalists: that is, they bought rugs from all of the rug-weaving areas. Since the 1960s the emphasis has shifted to collecting specific types. The major trend has been toward tribal and nomadic rugs, but many collectors focus on specific types such as Turkish, Caucasian, Turkoman, Afshar, donkeybags, prayer rugs, or kilims.

Collectors come from all walks of life. They may be corporate presidents or graduate students. They may buy only perfect-condition pieces or well-worn and tattered fragments. Many like to mix with other collectors, while some are reclusive and unknown except to a few dealers and auction houses. Some buy only from dealers, others only from auction houses, and many haunt house sales in their spare time. Some attend all conferences and some have never attended a conference. There is no one set of characteristics which sums up the Oriental rug collector. As with the rugs themselves, there are all kinds of exceptions to the "norm."

What collectors do all have in common is that they have to become experts in their field. They have to learn to identify the kinds of rug by design, technical features, type of wool, aesthetic qualities, and rarity. The ability to identify and evaluate are two skills they must develop as collectors.

HOW TO EVALUATE AN ANTIQUE ORIENTAL RUG

There are several general criteria that should be considered when inspecting a rug. These are:

▌ *Condition:* Is the rug complete; is the pile worn; are the edges unbroken; have there been losses to the ends of the rug; is there damage from moths or stains; have repairs been carried out?

▌ *Color:* Are the colors well matched, harmonious, and typical of the type; are the dyes all natural or are there synthetics; if there is abrash, does it add to or detract from the design?

▌ *Rarity:* Is the piece common for the type; are there many more like it or is it a one of a kind weaving?

▌ *Wool quality:* Is the wool typical of the type; is it soft/harsh, oily/dry, lustrous/dull and durable?

▌ *Function:* What was the rug's function – as a floor rug, bag, or festive trapping; is it a nomadic, village or city weaving?

▌ *Age:* Do the colors, design, condition, patterns, technical features, and wool conform to the age cited?

▌ *Aesthetic merit:* Do I personally find the color and design pleasing?

▌ *Price:* Is this reasonable, given the other factors; how soon will I see another example; is there basis for a "fair market value?"

ASSESSING THE MARKET VALUE OF AN ORIENTAL RUG

Every collector asks how he or she can assess the market value of a rug, but a precise answer is nowhere available. Old and antique Oriental rug prices are item-specific and their price can depend on where they are offered for sale – for instance, at a house sale or an auction or by a dealer. It may also vary depending on whether market prices are rising or falling; whether offered for sale in a city with many collectors or none; in a large city or small one; and whether collectors are interested in the type at the time. The market value of a given rug at a given point in time is reliably calculable only on new rugs where there is a known per-square-foot wholesale price. Old and antique rugs are best compared to paintings. Most people know that painting prices are highly variable, depending on these same types of factor.

Collectors who choose to rely on their own knowledge and expertise in buying rugs must attend auctions and subscribe to their catalogues to observe prices in that market. Dealers' quoted prices are another source of value information, as is attendance at trade fairs where old rugs are sometimes sold. Only by constantly being in touch with these resources can a collector have a sense of the price value of collectible Oriental rugs. Even then the estimated price of a given rug by knowledgeable collectors can vary greatly.

RIGHT **Konya prayer rug, 3ft. 10in. × 4ft. 5in., c. 1850. In design and color this rug typifies many Konya rugs: simple mihrab arch and clear red, good green, and bright yellow. The cartouche main border design derives from seventeenth-century rugs from Transylvania.**

PETER PAP ORIENTAL RUGS, INC. PHOTO GARY McKINNIS.

ABOVE **Ayaviçik rug, 4ft. 3in. × 5ft. 1in., woven 1991. Ayaviçik rugs are woven in the same region as those of the DOBAG project, but are sold without the trademark. Similar designs are used. Most Ayvaçiks have had a chemical wash to soften the colors.**

PETER PAP ORIENTAL RUGS, INC. PHOTO GARY McKINNIS.

PETER PAP ORIENTAL RUGS, INC.
PHOTO GARY McKINNIS.

A GUIDE FOR COLLECTORS

CHAPTER 10

Any type of collecting requires dedication, education, time, and money. The only way to avoid expending all but the latter is to find a dealer or auction house and rely on their advice. They can show you rugs which they have or inform you about others which are on the market. Most collectors, however, choose to do their own searching and buying from a variety of sources. For many "the pleasure is in the search."

To educate yourself about Oriental rugs involves reading, visiting dealers and auction houses to see quantities of rugs, meeting other collectors, visiting museums and exhibitions, and attending conferences on aspects of rugs not found in other sources. Some specific resources are listed below.

BOOKS, CATALOGS, AND PERIODICALS

Rug literature comes in several forms. It includes exhibition catalogs and books by experts on rugs in general or on specific types. In spite of the large number of publications on the subject, they are not easy to find in bookstores. Many go out of print quickly and never reach a wide audience. Most books on sale in shops are general surveys; to find more specialized literature you need to go to a library (though unfortunately most stock only a few books on Oriental rugs) or contact a specialist supplier. Most of the latter do their business by catalog sales, or mail order. Some who deal internationally are:

Myrna Bloom-East/West Room, 3139 Alpin Drive, Dresher, PA 19025

ABOVE LEFT **Baluchi saltbag, 11in. × 1ft. 8in., c. 1920. Baluchi flatweaves often display several different techniques; this saltbag has at least five. Saltbags of all groups are of this shape, but the size and** length of the neck vary considerably. This one has small areas of pink and yellow silk in the small crosses on the center border of the bottom area.

Dennis Marquand, PO Box 1187, Culver City, CA 90232

The Rug Book Shop, 2603 Talbot Road, Baltimore, MD 21216

International General, PO Box 305, New York, NY 10013

Abington Books, Little Abington, Cambridge CB1 6BQ UK

Uta Hulsey, Postfach 34, D–4230 Wesel, Germany

Only two periodicals are published for collectors of Oriental rugs. Both are bimonthly and are not available from newsstands. They are sold primarily by subscription. Since they differ considerably in content, most collectors subscribe to both. They are:

Oriental Rug Review, PO Box 709, Meredith, NH 03253

Hali Magazine, Kingsgate House, Kingsgate Place, London NW6 4TA, UK

DEALERS

Most people begin the process of learning about Oriental rugs with a dealer in old and antique rugs. Dealers are the source of information usually closest to where you live, they have an inventory of various types of rug and are usually willing to explain their qualities and technical features.

The ability to identify the different kinds of knot, degree of warp depression, types of edge finish, and so on is something collectors should aim to acquire, though obviously it is up to individuals to decide how far they want their learning to go. These factors are, after all, frequently the reason why rugs of similar type can vary by thousands of dollars in price. Most cities and towns do not offer courses on Oriental rugs on a regular basis, but dealers are usually willing to assume the role of teacher.

Many collectors find a dealer with whom they have a good rapport and trust. The dealer knows what types of rug interest them. When such rugs come along, they will bring them to the collector's attention. The dealer/collector relationship is one which needs to be carefully cultivated by both parties. Dealers want to sell; collectors want to acquire. Both parties need to keep this in mind.

PETER PAP ORIENTAL RUGS, INC. PHOTO GARY McKINNIS.

LEFT **Yomud torba, 1ft. × 2ft. 7in., c. 1890. Torbas are long, shallow bags. This one has the kepse gul and a typical Yomud border pattern. Remnants of the long fringe in blue and red can be seen at the bottom. The red and blue braided cords at the side were originally longer and secured the torba to the frame of the yurt.**

RUG SOCIETIES

Another way of learning is from other collectors. Most collectors like to know others in order to compare pieces and share knowledge. This is done through Oriental rug societies, which exist in the major cities of most countries. Rug societies meet a few times a year, when specialists talk about specific types of rugs and the members share information about their acquisitions. Collectors also learn at such meetings about dealers and exhibitions where Oriental rugs can be seen. Since rug prices can vary considerably, comparing prices is another aspect of these associations.

Information about rug societies and their activities is reported in the two periodicals listed on page 75. Museum curatorial staff and auction house specialists usually can provide the addresses of societies in their country or area.

MUSEUMS

Museums are the repositories of examples of most great rugs of the classical period. Some possess collections of rugs of more recent vintage. Museums with noteworthy collections are:

Victoria and Albert Museum, London, U.K.

Metropolitan Museum of Art, New York

Textile Museum, Washington D.C.

Museum of Art, Philadelphia, PA

City Art Museum, St Louis, MO

Museum of Fine Arts, San Francisco, CA

Museum of Islamic Art, Berlin, Germany

Museum für Angewandte Kunst, Vienna, Austria

Iparmuveszeti Museum, Budapest, Hungary

Gulbenkian Museum, Lisbon, Portugal

Turk ve Islam Eserleri Museum, Istanbul, Turkey

CONFERENCES AND EXHIBITIONS

Oriental rug conferences and exhibitions are held occasionally and sponsored by various organizations. The major conferences are sponsored by the Textile Museum, Washington D.C. (annually), the American Conference on Oriental Rugs (biennially) and the International Conference on Oriental Carpets (triennially in the U.S., U.K., and Europe in rotation). These conferences normally last from one to three days. They include academic programs, exhibitions, and some type of rug fair. Information about these conferences is announced in Oriental Rug Review and Hali Magazine (see page 75).

JOHN J. COLLINS JR. GALLERY.

LEFT **Bijar rug, 4ft. × 6ft. 2in., c. 1900. This piece shows a village weaver's attempt to weave the complex harshang pattern. The large palmettes and rosettes are here, but in a** more angular, less precise drawing. The corners illustrate the weaver's failed attempt at reconciled corners, a charming feature.

WHERE TO BUY

The most important decision in becoming an Oriental rug collector is buying the first rug. Not until you have one in your home can it be studied, felt by hand and foot, and integrated to determine how captivated you will be by Oriental rugs. Only in this way can you begin to sense what rug collecting is all about. In the long run the first purchase will either be loved for sentimental reasons or hated. It may be kept as a reminder of mistakes to be avoided or the first rug you sell.

Once the first purchase is made, decisions about what and where to buy in the future can be made. That decision will depend largely on your personality, time, special interests, where you live, and your budget.

DEALERS

Dealers are one of the major sources of antique Oriental rugs. Although there has been a resurgence of interest in rug collecting in the past twenty-five years, there has not been a concomitant increase in the number of dealers. The vast majority of dealers sell new rugs; only a few specialize in old and antique ones, and most are in large cities.

AUCTIONS

Auctions are another important source not only for buying but also for seeing many rugs at one time. Many of the major auction houses in most countries hold specialized sales of Oriental rugs, which may be viewed for one or more days beforehand. Viewing is a good way to familiarize yourself with a wide variety of rugs. A dealer rarely has an inventory equal to that of a major sale. During this time you can inspect the rugs for condition and wear. Advice on what a rug may sell for is available from the house specialist. But you can never be sure what price a rug will fetch at auction until the auctioneer says "Sold." Auction purchases cannot be returned and are *caveat emptor* ("let the buyer beware").

PETER PAP ORIENTAL RUGS, INC.

ABOVE **Kuba rug, 3ft. 10in. × 6ft., c. 1880. The interlocking pattern of the main border of this rug is closely identified with Caucasian rugs, although it occurs in some Persian tribal rugs as well. However, the spacious drawing and color juxtapositions are particularly effective.**

SHORT-NOTICE SALES

Short-notice sales take various forms. They may be house sales where an entire estate is being sold or itinerant rug auctions at a local hotel. Whatever type, if you want to buy, you must be very knowledgeable to avoid making a bad financial mistake.

At house sales the rugs may be underpriced or overpriced. Some collectors have found great rugs in this way, but just as many have taken a rug home from such a sale and discovered cat or dog urine, moth damage, or that it has been reduced in length.

At short-notice auctions most of the rugs are new and many have problems. The viewing is usually short without sufficient time to inspect the rugs. When the bidding starts, there are sometimes false bidders who work with the auctioneer to drive the prices up. Although fifty to a hundred rugs may be bid for and appear to have been sold during the auction, only a few actually are sold.

SELECT BIBLIOGRAPHY

The following books are intended as a guide for those who wish to explore the world of Oriental rugs in greater depth. Many of them are still in print.

Those not in print are usually available from the dealers in Oriental rug books. The most highly recommended books have been marked with an asterisk.

GENERAL BOOKS

*EILAND, MURRAY *Oriental Rugs, a Comprehensive Guide*, Little, Brown and Co., Boston, 1981.

*HUBEL, REINHARD B., *The Book of Carpets*, Praeger Publishers, New York, 1970.

JACOBSEN, CHARLES W., *Oriental Rugs, a Complete Guide*, Charles E. Tuttle Co. Rutland, VT, 1962.

JERREHIAN, ARAM, *Oriental Rug Primer*, Running Press, New York, 1980.

SPUHLER, F., KONIG, H., AND VOLKMANN, M., *Old Eastern Carpets/ Alte Orientteppiche*, Verlag Callwey, Munich, 1978.

STANZER, WILFRED, ET AL., *Antique Oriental Carpets from Austrian Collections/Antike Orientteppiche aus Osterreichischem Besitz*, Society for Textile Art Research, Vienna, 1986.

*THOMPSON, JON, *Oriental Carpets from the Tents, Cottages and Workshops of Asia*, E. P. Dutton, New York, 1988.

VOLKMANN, MARTIN, ET AL, *Old Eastern Carpets/Alte Orientteppiche*, Verlag Callwey, Munich, 1985.

RUGS OF TURKEY

*BRUGGEMANN, W., AND BOHMER, H., *Rugs of the Peasants and Nomads of Anatolia*, Kunst & Antiquitaten, Munich, 1983.

BRUGGEMANN, WERNER, *Yayla, Form und Farbe in Turkischer Textilkunst*, Museum für Islamische Kunst, Berlin, 1993.

ZIPPER, KURT AND FRITZSCHE, CLAUDIA, *Oriental Rugs*, Vol. 4 *Turkish*, Battenburg Verlag, Munich, 1989.

RUGS OF THE CAUCASUS

*BENNETT, IAN, *Oriental Rugs*, Vol. 1 *Caucasian*, Oriental Textiles Press, Woodbridge, U.K., 1981.

ELLIS, CHARLES GRANT, *Early Caucasian Rugs*, Textile Museum, Washington D.C., 1975.

SCHURMANN, ULRICH, *Caucasian Rugs*, George Allen & Unwin, London, 1965.

YETKIN, SERARE, *Early Caucasian Carpets in Turkey*, Vols. 1 and 2, Oguz Press, London, 1978.

RUGS OF IRAN

EDWARDS, A. CECIL, *The Persian Carpet*, Duckworth Ltd, London, 1975.

GANS-REUDIN, E., *The Splendor of Persian Carpets*, Rizzoli, New York, 1978.

OPIE, JAMES, *Tribal Rugs of Southern Persia*, James Opie Oriental Rugs, Portland, OR, 1981.

RUGS OF CENTRAL ASIA

JOURDAN, UWE, *Orientteppiche*, Band 4 *Turkmenische Teppiche*, Battenburg Verlag, Munich, 1989.

*MACKIE, LOUISE AND THOMPSON, JON, *Turkmen Tribal Carpets and Traditions*, Textile Museum, Washington D.C., 1980.

O'BANNON, GEORGE W., ET AL., *Vanishing Jewels, Central Asian Tribal Weavings*, Rochester Museum and Science Center, Rochester, New York, 1990.

PARSONS, R. D., *Oriental Rugs*, Vol. 3 *The Carpets of Afghanistan* Oriental Textiles Press, Woodbridge, UK, 1983.

TSAREVA, ELENA, *Rugs and Carpets from Central Asia, The Russian Collections*, Allen Lane/Penguin Books, New York, 1984.

RUGS OF CHINA, TIBET, AND EAST TURKESTAN

BIDDER, HANS, *Carpets from Eastern Turkestan*, Universe Books, New York, 1984.

EILAND, MURRAY, *Chinese and Exotic Rugs*, New York Graphic Society, Boston, 1979.

*LARSSON, LENNART, *Carpets from China, Xinjiang and Tibet*, Bamboo Publ. Ltd, London, 1988.

MYERS, DIANA K., *Temple, Household Horseback: Rugs of the Tibetan Plateau,* Textile Museum, Washington D.C., 1984.

*****ROSTOV, CHARLES I.,** AND **GUANYAN, JIA,** *Chinese Carpets,* Harry N. Abrams, New York, 1983.

RUGS OF SPECIFIC GROUPS

BLACK, DAVID, AND **LOVELESS, CLIVE,** *Rugs of the Wandering Baluch,* David Black Oriental Carpets, London, 1976.

BOUCHER, JEFF, *Baluchi Woven Treasures,* Jeff W. Boucher, Alexandria, VA, 1989.

CRAYCRAFT, MICHAEL, *Belouch Prayer Rugs,* Adraskand Galleries, Point Reyes Station, CA, 1982.

*****EAGLETON, WILLIAM,** *An Introduction to Kurdish Rugs and Other Weavings,* Interlink Books, New York, 1988.

LANDREAU, ANTHONY N., *Yoruk, the Nomadic Weaving Tradition of the Middle East,* Carnegie Museum of Art, Pittsburgh, 1978.

OPIE, JAMES, *Tribal Rugs,* Tolstoy Press, Portland, OR, 1992.

REINISCH, HELMUT, *Saddle Bags/ Satteltaschen,* Verlag für Sammler, Graz, Austria, 1985.

REINISCH, HELMUT, *Gabbeh, the Georges D. Bornet Collection,* Helmut Reinisch, Graz, Austria, 1986.

SCHLAMMINGER, KARL, AND **WILSON, P. L.,** *Weaver of Tales, Persian Picture Rugs/Persische Bildteppich,* Callwey Verlag, Munich, 1980.

STANZER, WILFRIED, *Kordi, Lives- Rugs-Flatweaves of the Kurds in Khorasan,* Adil Besim, Vienna, 1988.

*****TANAVOLI, PARVIZ,** *Shahsavan, Iranian Rugs and Textiles,* Rizzoli, New York, 1985.

FLATWOVEN RUGS

BALPINAR, BELKIS, AND **HIRSCH, UDO,** *Flatweaves of the Vakiflar Museum, Istanbul,* Uta Hulsey Verlag, Wesel, Germany, 1982.

BORALEVI, ALBERTO, *Sumakh, Flatwoven Carpets of the Caucasus,* Karta SAS, Florence, 1986.

COOTNER, CATHRYN, M., *The Arthur D. Jenkins Collection,* Vol. 1 *Flatwoven Textiles,* Textile Museum, Washington D.C., 1981.

*****DAVIES, PETER,** *The Tribal Eye, Antique Kilims of Anatolia,* Rizzoli, New York, 1993.

*****HULL, ALASTAIR,** AND **LUCZYC- WYHOWSKA, JOSE,** *Kilim, The Complete Guide,* Thames and Hudson, London, 1993.

JUSTIN, VALERIE, *Flat-woven Rugs of the World, Kilim, Soumak and Brocading,* Van Nostrand Reinhold Co., New York, 1980.

LANDREAU, ANTHONY L., AND **PICKERING, W. R.,** *From Bosporus to Samarkand, Flat-woven Rugs,* Textile Museum, Washington D.C., 1969.

PETSOPOULOS, YANNI, *Kilims, Flat- woven Tapestry Rugs,* Rizzoli, New York, 1979.

DESIGNS AND PATTERNS

ETTINGHAUSEN, R., DIMAND, M., AND **MACKIE, L.,** *Prayer Rugs,* Textile Museum, Washington D.C., 1974.

*****FORD, J. P. J.,** *The Oriental Carpet, History and Guide to Motifs, Patterns and Symbols,* Harry N. Abrams, New York, 1981.

STONE, PETER F., *Rugs of the Caucasus: Structure and Design,* Greenleaf Co., Chicago, 1984.

MUSEUM AND PRIVATE COLLECTIONS

BALPINAR, BELKIS, AND **HIRSCH, UDO,** *Carpets of the Vakiflar Museum Istanbul,* Uta Hulsey Verlag, Wesel, Germany, 1988.

*****BEATTIE, MAY H.,** *The Thyssen- Bornemisza Collection of Oriental Rugs,* Villa Favorita, Castagnola, Italy, 1972.

DIMAND, MAURICE S., AND **MAILEY, JEAN,** *Oriental Rugs in the Metropolitan Museum of Art,* Metropolitan Museum of Art, New York, 1973.

EILAND, MURRAY, *Oriental Rugs from Pacific Collections,* San Francisco Bay Area Rug Society, San Francisco, 1990.

*****ELLIS, CHARLES GRANT,** *Oriental Carpets in the Philadelphia Museum of Art,* Museum of Art, Philadelphia, 1988.

SPUHLER, FRIEDRICH, *Oriental Carpets in the Museum of Islamic Art, Berlin,* Smithsonian Institution, Washington DC, 1987.

OTHER ASPECTS OF ORIENTAL RUG DEVELOPMENT, HISTORY, AND CARE

BARBER, E. J. R., *Prehistoric Textiles, The Development of Cloth in the Neolithic and Bronze Age,* Princeton University Press, Princeton, NJ, 1991.

STONE, PETER F., *Oriental Rug Repair,* Greenleaf Co., Chicago, 1981.

*****WARE, JOYCE C.,** *The Official Identification and Price Guide Oriental Rugs,* House of Collectibles, New York, 1992.

INDEX

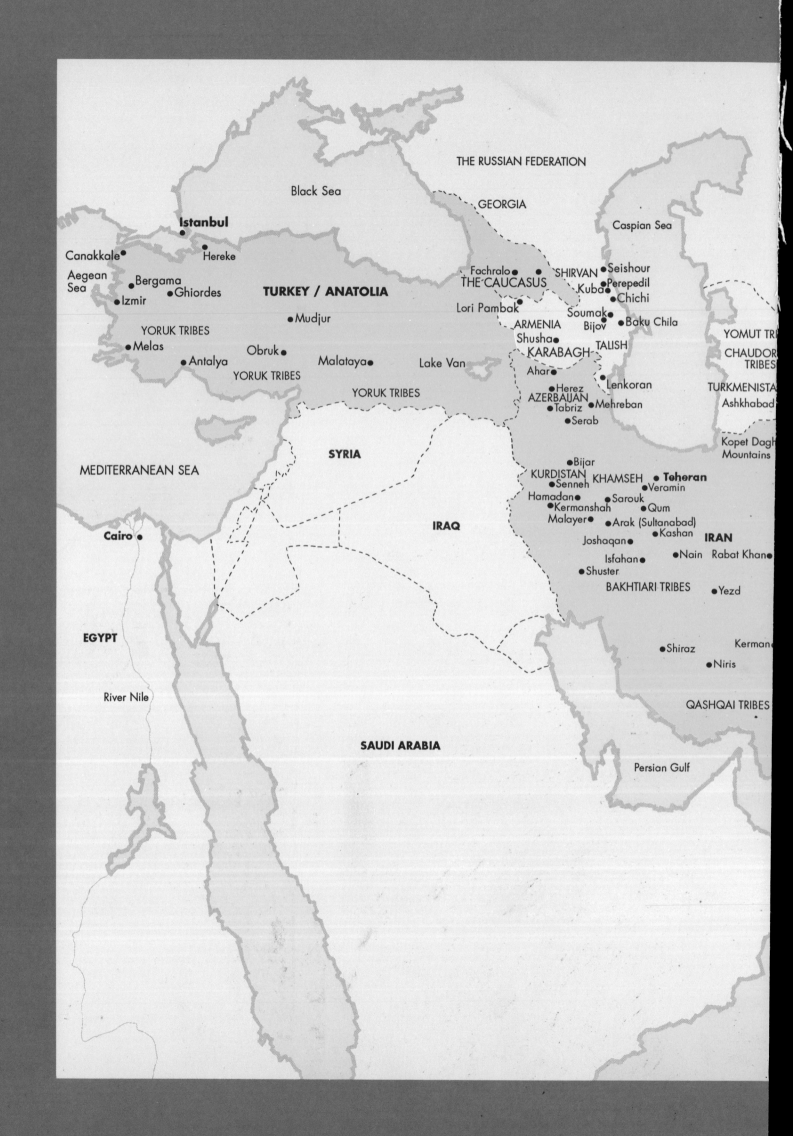